[ENDORSEMENTS]

Many people want to talk about what it means to live life with margin and freedom, but far fewer actually do it. Tommy Thompson knows firsthand the allure of a life of busyness and the high cost to our souls. With wisdom, gentleness, and clarity, he guides us from the hurried and frantic life of lack to the beautiful and good life of abundance. As I read the book, I found myself encouraged and inspired to discover how a life with space to breathe is the full and free life I've been seeking.

Nicole Unice, pastor, leadership coach
and author of several books, including *The Struggle is Real: Getting Better at Life, Stronger in Faith, and Free From the Stuff that's Keeping You Stuck*

Tommy and I have had a rich friendship for thirty years, including vacations and Christmas dinners as family. We have talked, counseled, laughed, cried, prayed, and played together, experiencing the ups and downs in some of life's most joyful and most painful places. We have had the privilege of a weekly breakfast now for twenty-eight years. In *Space to Breathe Again*, Tommy speaks authentically about seeking a life of meaning with an invitation to join him, not as one who has arrived, but as one who is paying attention, intent on growing, and doing it with openness and humility. If you are looking for more meaning and less anxiety in life, I'm glad you're reading *Space to Breathe Again*.

David Dwight, co-author of *Start Here and the Way*
Senior Pastor of Hope Church, Richmond, VA

SPACE TO

[BREATHE]
Again

Hope for the Overloaded and Overwhelmed

Tommy Thompson

Mary Mary maret,
Thanks so much for your help!
Tammy
Matt. 11:28-29

Creative Enterprises Studio

Bedford, TX

Published in association with Books, Bach & Beyond, Inc. d/b/a Creative Enterprises Studio, 1507 Shirley Way, Bedford, TX 76022. CreativeEnterprisesStudio.com.

Unless otherwise noted, Scripture quotations are taken from the Holy Bible, New International Version®, NIV®. Copyright © 1973, 1978, 1984, 2011 by Biblica, Inc.™ Used by permission of Zondervan. All rights reserved worldwide. www.zondervan.com. The "NIV" and "New International Version" are trademarks registered in the United States Patent and Trademark Office by Biblica, Inc.™

Scripture quotations marked THE MESSAGE are taken from *The Message*. Copyright © by Eugene H. Peterson 1993, 1994, 1995, 1996, 2000, 2001, 2002. Used by permission of Tyndale House Publishers, Inc.

Scripture quotations marked NASB are taken from the New American Standard Bible®, Copyright © 1960, 1962, 1963, 1968, 1971, 1972, 1973, 1975, 1977, 1995 by The Lockman Foundation. Used by permission. (www.Lockman.org)

Scripture quotations marked NIV® are taken from the New International Reader's Version (NIrV) Copyright © 1995, 1996, 1998, 2014 by Biblica, Inc.®. Used by permission. All rights reserved worldwide, www.zondervan.com. The "NIrV" and "New International Reader's Version" are trademarks registered in the United States Patent and Trademark Office by Biblica, Inc.®

Scripture quotations marked NKJV are taken from the New King James Version®. Copyright © 1982 by Thomas Nelson. Used by permission. All rights reserved.

Scripture quotations marked NLT are taken from the Holy Bible, New Living Translation, copyright © 1996, 2004, 2007, 2013 by Tyndale House Foundation. Used by permission of Tyndale House Publishers, Inc., Carol Stream, Illinois 60188. All rights reserved.

Library of Congress Cataloging-in-Publication Data

ISBN Softcover: 978-1-7349400-0-8
    Hardcover: 978-1-7349400-2-2
    Audio Book: 978-0-578-7351-3-9
    e-Book: 978-1-7349400-1-5

Cover Design: StudioAnneli.com
Interior Design: Inside-Out Design & Typesetting

Printed in the United States of America

20 21 22 23 24 25   VP   6 5 4 3 2 1

[CONTENTS]

[CONTENTS]

[CONTENTS]

[DEDICATION]

To Perrin,

How could one so young teach us so much? You taught us courage through years and years of living vibrantly in spite of fear. You taught us joy in the midst of pain and constant suffering. You taught us faith, never wavering in your confidence in God, even though your every day was a challenge. Your smile lit up the room.

You are so deeply missed and forever loved!

Dad

[ACKNOWLEDGMENTS]

My thanks go so far beyond those special people who helped me with this book. I have been the recipient of so much encouragement with my teaching and writing over the years. From the very first time I taught about "margin," countless friends told me that this mattered. They patted me on the back and wrote notes urging me to keep on following my passion for impacting people for good and for God. The church communities of Third Church and Hope Church have not only cheered me along the way but have shaped who I am as a teacher and follower of Jesus.

Beyond this, though, when life turned upside down the day Perrin was diagnosed with cancer, my friends and family proved that their love went beyond mere words. My parents were remarkable as they suffered along with our family. My siblings, Elizabeth, Mike, and Litt, supported us each step of the long journey. Friends brought countless meals, wrote love-filled notes, and astounded us with creative acts of love.

Close friends have walked with me through life's darkest days, described in these pages. Randall White, David Dwight, Ron Klipp, and Steve Hartman held me up when I could not stand on my own. Their friendship colors my bias that relationships are the place where joy is found.

Thank you to all not mentioned by name who have loved our family in this season of pain.

The day I put the first draft of this manuscript in the hands of intelligent, thoughtful, truthful, and, most important, graceful friends was terrifying. Would they come back with feigned interest, harsh criticism, even discouragement? I relied on my friends' grace and truth: Patricia Clarke, Steve Perkins, Shawn Boyer, Karen

[ACKNOWLEDGMENTS]

Hayes, JG Carter, and Rachel Dawson. Each of you read the draft through different lenses that provided much-needed perspective. You will never know how much your insightful comments and suggestions affected the final form of *Space to Breathe Again*. Some chapters rightly never saw the light of day. Other chapters benefited from needed expansion. Adverbs were ditched, structure made clearer, judgmental statements avoided. Perhaps most important, your honest encouragement stoked my resolve to finish this book that had been in the works for so long.

My utmost gratitude extends also to many creative voices who have helped me along this journey. Paige Daniels's photography, Drew Daniels's and Joe Wise's assistance with my podcasting efforts in which many of these ideas have been tested, and AJ Roberts's incredible cover concept add immeasurably to the words written.

I never could have brought this book to print without the incredible assistance of Mary Hollingsworth and her team at Creative Enterprises Studio. Special thanks to Renee Chavez for her expert eye sifting through the manuscript with needed edits, and others on the team who brought their talents to the work.

Finally, my family is my rock. Chris and Alex, Perrin's brothers, endured all of the last ten years with strength unimaginable. It has not been easy. They are men of character, compassion, and love. They will be leaving quite a mark on this world in the years to come. Both Alex and Chris have helped me each step of the way as I learn to write. They are faithful readers of endless blogs and awkward social media posts, and through their constant ribbing, they keep me humble. They regularly help me see through the eyes of millennials, as I hope that these thoughts help across all ages.

Weezie stands above them all. She is my love, my editor, my encourager, my faithful follower. We have walked this road together as we learned to create space to breathe. Her depth of faith inspires me. Writing a book pales next to the journey we walked through together with Perrin. Weezie's love and heart and compassion showed me God's love and heart and compassion. I am so thankful that God brought us together more than forty years ago.

[INTRODUCTION]

I have such an overwhelming sense of gratefulness at bringing this book to life, not only because this is my first book. My heart and life are in this book. Life lived over the last thirty years fill its pages. Occasional triumph and buckets of tears coarse through these years and these pages.

I am learning how to write and how to live. This book describes the lessons learned in the crucible of experiences that I never would have imagined. The number of course corrections tried and gleaned from are more than I can count. My hope and prayer are that my lessons learned in the dark and in the light might help you in the practicality of your days.

This gets at my strong desire. I want my words to be practical and usable. Certainly, I hope they will also be thought-provoking and inspirational; but inspiration that cannot be used only puffs us up for a few moments.

Throughout this book I will offer practical suggestions that you can put into practice. In the midst of an entire book, though, ideas can overwhelm to the point that nothing changes. My encouragement with *Space to Breathe Again* is to start your journey by using this book as a resource to experiment. In chapters where I offer several tips, pick only one. You can always come back for more later. If the end result of your reading this book is one or two practical changes that take deep root for your lifetime, my highest dreams would be realized.

Let's Get Personal

I have decided in this book to get personal. To that end, I am introducing you to my family. Rather than refer to "my wife," as if you do not know me, I will talk about Weezie. We have been married for thirty-eight years. She is wonderful, and I don't want to write about her as if she is a random person. My sons are Chris and Alex. You will hear about them also. My daughter, Perrin, is no longer with us on this earth. You will hear about her magnificent walk and the extraordinary lessons she taught me through the way she lived her life.

This book describes a journey, not an arrival. I do not pretend to have my act together. Like Thomas Edison, who found thousands of ways *not* to create a light bulb,[1] my tendency to take on more than I can manage has forced me to try ten thousand ways to create space and rhythm. In the process of that trial and error, a few strategies surfaced that work.

If, on occasion, I express my convictions in ways that come across as insensitive to the magnitude of overload that exists in your life, please forgive me. I remember all too well what it feels like to be drowning and have simple platitudes offered by someone in an easier season of life. If you disagree or think I am being naive and impractical, I'd love to hear your thoughts. Consider this the first part of a conversation. We grow through open conversation.

Finally, I write this book from a faith perspective, because that is the landscape in which I have lived my life. My faith is the foundation of all that I do and think, but I am aware that others do not see the world as I do. I hope that if that describes you, you will continue to read further, not because I will try to convince you of my way of thinking, but because we are all on a road together and life is hard, and we need each other. You may learn from my journey as I know I would learn from yours.

In the end, our world will be better if a few of us seek to change the tide of striving and overload and begin to breathe again the air of joy and contentment and deep relationship.

How to Read *Space to Breathe Again*

Space to Breathe Again is designed intentionally to be read easily and slowly. I am a voracious reader, but I have found as I get older that

I have a shorter attention span when I read. Perhaps this is the fruit of a culture that is constantly chipping away at everyone's attention span. Regardless, I have written each chapter with subchapters that can be absorbed in a short amount of time. The lessons have a clear order, but they can be consumed out of order or with breaks in between. The hope is that this will make reading easier and also allow you space to mull over what you have read and even answer a few of the questions.

Breathing exercises are included throughout the book as practical ways of testing and more deeply exposing the concepts. For those so inclined, these will help make the leap from conceptual to the actual activities of daily life. These breathing exercises are ways to break through the hard exterior of set patterns.

At the end of each chapter, I include a summary called "Key Takeaways." Most of the time, when I read a book on my Kindle, I highlight the book in such a way that after I finish, I am able to copy the highlights, paste them into a document, and be most of the way toward an outline. This helps me better learn and internalize the content. These key takeaways will make this easier as well as be a way to refresh the thoughts from the previous pages.

Finally, I have an assortment of tools and additional resources available online at www.tommythompson.org/SpacetoBreatheAgain. I refer to many of these resources in the pages ahead but look forward to adding new resources to facilitate the ongoing conversation of how we find the life-giving rhythm that God intended.

For those who want a deeper dive, I encourage you to read this book with a journal close by. Certain places will mean more if you mull over your own personal experience. Other places will need a pause so you can decide what, practically, you will implement. Whether you read the book straight through, as I do with most books I read, or take your time, my desire is that it will have even a fraction of the impact on your life that these life lessons have had on mine.

[PART ONE]

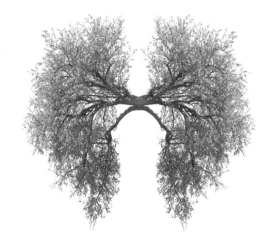

Overloaded and Overwhelmed

[1]
Breathless

There are endless possibilities waiting for us, much of the life that
God longs for us to live is just one choice away.

—Erwin McManus, *Seizing Your Divine Moment*

Runaway Train

How did life get so out of control? It's almost as if we are on a
train that starts off chugging along the tracks, slowly gaining
speed. We hear the rhythm of the wheels turning faster and
faster, and we settle back in our seats, knowing we will get to our
destination on time. Then the train continues to speed up. Now,
the train is moving too fast, and we know something is wrong. We
wonder whether it can stay on the tracks at this speed. This train
ride is not what we bargained for. We are now hurtling down the
rails, with no way of stopping, destined to crash and burn.

Overload is like the train that is going faster and faster with no
way to stop. Escaping overload seems impossible, even as it snow-
balls more and more out of control. Slowing down and living a purposeful, balanced life feels utterly unrealistic. It would be nice, but
we can't imagine how to navigate without 24/7 availability. Smartphones, stressful jobs, and endless demands control our lives. The
only option, if we want to keep up with the world around us, is to
speed up. If we don't, we will get steamrolled.

To make matters worse, we know that in five years, today's pace
will seem like a stroll. Keeping our head above water feels daunt-
ing; getting ahead is another matter. We strive to prepare for college

educations, pay for weddings and vacations, and fund retirement. There is simply not enough time, money, and overall bandwidth to juggle all the balls required in today's world.

People deal differently with the saturated reality that we all fight. Some people strut proudly, complaining about their breathless lives, tinted with a bit of pride because they are obviously so indispensable. They claim that it is irresponsible to live such a comfortable life. Somehow, a person who is not always rushing, who does not always have more than can be reasonably handled, is seen as wasting his or her God-given talents. Christians can be the worst about this. A subtle spiritual barometer is held up, measuring the number of activities and the amount of sacrifice made in the name of Christ. Rarely do we ever consider boundaries regarding the amount of time one "devotes" to the church. The unspoken message is that we can do it all, we can have it all, and we need not ever limit ourselves. We hear, "I can do all things through Christ who strengthens me" (Phil. 4:13 NKJV). How ironic that we justify a hectic way of life characterized by overcommitment using words written by the apostle Paul when he was in prison, with little ability to do more than think, pray, and write.

Others struggle with a sense of drowning in overload, on the verge of tears, edging toward depression. They move in a zombielike state from one activity to another, perpetually exhausted, wondering if anything will ever change. They give up optimism for today, placing their fleeting hopes in vacations, an empty nest, and retirement, times they imagine when the pace might slow down. Their language is peppered with phrases such as "I can't wait until . . . ," "If only . . . ," and "I wish that . . ."

Christian philosopher Dallas Willard said two things that will always stick with me. When his good friend John Ortberg, pastor of a large church, came to him for advice on how to handle the overwhelming responsibilities he faced, Willard replied, "Ruthlessly eliminate hurry from your life." When pressed for additional sage advice, Willard simply repeated, "Ruthlessly eliminate hurry from your life."[1]

Willard's second comment that stopped me in my tracks came toward the end of his life, when someone asked him, "What one word would you use to describe Jesus?" I remember as I first read this story, that I began to imagine what Willard might say. The words *holy, joyful, humble* came to my mind as I imagined how I measured up. Willard replied, "Relaxed."[2] I was stunned as I read that word. The more I think about it, the more it fits. Jesus never rushed. He never seemed stressed except, understandably, in the Garden of Gethsemane. He cared deeply and always had time for people. Relaxed. Then I realized that I could hardly think of a word that described me less than "relaxed." I am driven and responsible—but *relaxed*?

Finally, there are those people who simply do not want to change. They may justify this by claiming that it is irresponsible or unrealistic to have breathing room, but the truth is that they do not want to change. They thrive on constant stimulation. Busyness creates a sense of worth and importance. Deep down, these well-intentioned people reason that if they are not busy, it must be because they are not needed. They are afraid of boredom and terrified of silence. Therefore, they feed themselves with a glut of tasks that make them feel vital and alive. They quip about the incredible number of emails they are forced to process, as their chests puff out a little. They breathlessly complain about how many hours they work each week, and then fill their weekends with even crazier schedules.

How do I know this? Because this is the story of much of my life over the past thirty years. On too many occasions I have proudly, breathlessly told friends how busy I am. On too many nights I have fallen into bed, exhausted beyond words. I thrive on stimulation and the accompanying sense of importance.

Though I am stubborn, God has patiently taught me over the past few decades how to create space to breathe again. I am imperfect in my practice, but I am moving in the right direction. More days have peaceful flow. The surprising consequence of slowing the runaway train filled with worry, distraction, and activities taking me nowhere is soul-satisfying purpose, life-giving relationship, and growing intimacy with God.

We are not destined to stay on the runaway train. We can choose to live differently. For some people, a few well-considered changes will slow the train to a manageable pace. For others, the magnitude of overload will require disembarking totally from the runaway train and choosing an altogether new train going in a different direction. The work we will do in the pages ahead will allow us each to discern the path we need to take to create space to breathe again.

BREATHING EXERCISE

Relaxing is more than vegetating or zoning out in front of a screen. Relaxing is enjoyable, refreshing, recuperating. Relaxing restores the soul. Make a list of the ways that you relax.

The Long Journey Down the Less-Traveled Road

I remember that night just after Christmas 1990 as if it were yesterday. At the time, I was the poster child of someone who was living the good life. At the same time, I was about to crash and burn. After receiving my master of divinity degree in the mid-'80s, I switched directions and decided to go into business with my brother. In a matter of a few years, we moved from running one small business to operating four small companies. Our main business, a chain of retail stores that we bought in the spring of 1989, was suffering the effects of our lack of experience in the retail industry, coupled with the beginnings of a severe recession. Sales were off, and the pressure was mounting. On top of this escalating time bomb at work, I taught a large Sunday school class at our church each week, was an elder, co-chaired a search committee, and watched out for the other three businesses. Every minute of every day shouted its demands at me. As I lay in bed in the middle of the night, wide-eyed, our new one-year-old, Perrin, slept in the next room.

I wondered how I'd gotten myself into this mess. My breathing became shallower and shallower, and I could feel myself spiraling down in the darkness, with no way out.

I couldn't make everyone happy. I wasn't even sure I could survive the onslaught that seemed to be attacking from every angle. I was miserable and felt on the verge of a nervous breakdown. If someone had told me in those dark days about the abundant life Jesus offered, I may have screamed.

I woke in the morning, clouded with despair. I plodded through the days ahead, determined to survive but not knowing which way to turn. Shortly after that night, when everything seemed to be unraveling, I came across the book *Margin* by Richard Swenson. He defines margin as "the space between our load and our limits. . . . Margin is the gap between rest and exhaustion, the space between breathing freely and suffocating."[3] Swenson wrote in the first chapter, "Why do so many of us feel like air-traffic controllers out of control?"[4] Throughout the book, he paints a picture of breathless people living perpetually overloaded lives. I saw clearly for the first time that my desire to have it all and do it all wasn't working. "Too much" was suffocating any semblance of life. Strangely, seeing the problem in all its gory detail gave me hope that change was possible.

I initially thought creating margin in my life would be a simple process. I found the challenge much more complicated than I anticipated. While I wanted to get off the speeding train, the train didn't want to slow down. The leaps of progress that I hoped for were only baby steps. Many baby steps, though, made an impact. Hope raised its head. I began to catch my breath for the first time in a long, long time.

My wife, Weezie, felt the onslaught too. We decided together to push back against the riptide urging us toward more. We started small by adding a few things that we knew we desperately needed and taking away other time-wasters. We inserted a morning quiet time into our daily routine. With new resolve, we woke earlier and began our days with undisturbed time with God. The calm of the morning began to leak into the chaos of the day. We de-committed from every commitment that we could responsibly stop, and purposefully worked to slow the pace of our evenings. Even though it didn't feel like we could afford the time, we committed to practicing the Sabbath, one day of rest, as God commanded.

Each year we eked out a little more space, and we began to find sanity. The businesses slowly settled down. The family grew in size. We seemed to do less than those around us but be happier in our less.

As a teacher at our church, I began telling others about this concept of finding life through less. I found that people from all walks of life, from every conceivable circumstance, were drowning from overload. They sighed an audible sigh of relief when I spoke of a better way, where we could breathe again and change the way we lived.

The sun slowly began to shine again, and hope rose high. We found that with great effort and intentionality, it was possible to lead a full, purposeful life without caving in to the demands of a saturated culture. We were learning to prosper with less. Little did we know how valuable these lessons would be as a storm quickly descended on us.

BREATHING EXERCISE

Margin, when it comes to our lives, is not only about having fewer things but about having the right things. Name one thing that you need to add into your life. Name one thing that you need to delete from your life.

The Fateful Call

The call came at 3:00 p.m. on Thursday, March 4, 2010. Weezie left early that morning and drove six hours to be with Perrin, our daughter, who was a sophomore in college and was having extreme back pain. She was scheduled for an MRI, suspecting a herniated disk. When I answered the phone, Weezie simply said, "Perrin has lymphoma." The MRI had uncovered a large mass on her spine. The doctor was 99 percent certain the tumor was malignant. Perrin had been scheduled to leave the next day on a spring break trip, but instead packed her bags to come home from college to face her cancer.

Three days later, she checked into the hospital to see what lay ahead. The doctor had assured us that lymphoma was eminently treatable. Once she checked in to her room, the hospital did a routine CT scan to assess the extent of the cancer.

That afternoon, the doctor came into our roomful of visitors with a rattled look. He made small talk for a minute among the visitors and left the room. I could sense that something was wrong and quietly followed him to find out what was going on. He told me that the CT scans showed that the cancer was not lymphoma, but kidney cancer, a devastating diagnosis. When kidney cancer metastasizes, as it had with Perrin, there is no cure. The survival stats were horrific. He tried to encourage us by saying that new treatments were being tested, and that if we could just keep the cancer at bay, then perhaps there was still hope.

Our lives were turned upside down. We began a six-and-a-half-year journey with Perrin through the worst nightmare a parent could face. She endured multiple surgeries, five different forms of chemotherapy, various radiation protocols, and new, cutting-edge immunotherapy.

Despite constant pain and the side effects of terrible drugs, she experienced more joy and life in her six and a half years than most people do in a lifetime. In spite of suffering constant sickness and pain from the cancer and its treatments, she eventually graduated college. One of those summers she traveled to France with Weezie. In the middle of that six-plus-year battle, she married an incredible man, Joe Hall, she had met in her last two years of college. A year later, Weezie and I joined the newlyweds on a weeklong trip to Ireland. She loved everyone with whom she came into contact: nurses, hospital attendants, friends who came to comfort her. With all of her cancer-ridden being, she never lost hope. In an article she wrote for the Faith and Values section of the *Washington Post* in 2012 she affirmed, "Cancer has been a turning point in my life that I never could have dreamed of, and I know that my life will never be the same. But despite the hard times and the multitudes of tears, the Lord has been protecting me every step of this journey. Whether I live, and one day become cancer-free, or I die, I know without a doubt that God is good, and that does not change based on my circumstances."[5]

Perrin died on November 25, 2016.

[ ]

Before that call in March 2010, my life was full of the usual surprises that come with raising a family while running multiple businesses. One week a call came about an ailing parent who needed attention. The next week a son caught an elbow while playing basketball and got a freak concussion. Then a hot business opportunity threw the equilibrium off. Every week had its stresses.

Almost two decades of hyperfocus on creating space in our lives helped us keep that usual chaos to a barely manageable level. Of course, we did not see the storm that came out of nowhere. No one ever does. Crazy as it sounds, although nothing could prepare us for the pain and suffering that would become our everyday existence, the work to create some reasonable margin in our lives over the previous decades allowed us to immediately batten down the hatches for what lay ahead.

After the initial onslaught of surgeries and doctors' appointments, I went to my brother, who was my business partner, and completely changed my work identity. I asked him, at a crucial time in the company's future, if I could back off indefinitely. I said that I didn't want to leave him in the lurch. I would do those things that I, and only I, could do, but no more. I would take whatever cut in pay was necessary. My priorities had changed! Of course, he gave me full permission to do whatever I had to do for my family. I will forever be thankful to him and so many others who gave me the freedom to attend to what was most important.

The crazy thing was that even though my time decreased by over 50 percent, I honestly think that I maintained 80 percent of my effectiveness. I stopped shuffling papers and doing tasks that seemed important but, in reality, were not critical.

At the same time, I doubled the time I spent each morning with God. I was desperate to quiet the screaming voices of fear inside me. While I was tempted to run from quiet, I chose to embrace quiet as a means to make space for God to help me. These were not pretty mornings. I cried a lot and journaled my pain and fear. The time allowed me to honestly face the question, "Why me?" I could then move beyond that to focus on "What do I need to hear?" Those early-morning times were precious to both Weezie and me. They were our lifeline.

As soon as the news of Perrin's cancer became public, we were inundated with love and support, for which we will always be grateful. While that outpouring meant the world to us, it also created a mountain of intense conversations and an even more massive mountain of tasks thanking all those who cared for us. We knew we had to have boundaries. We did what we could do, and no more. Our emotions were raw, and we had to give those emotions breathing room, or we would have exploded.

We intentionally leaned in to a few friends. For me, three friends held me up when I could not stand on my own. These were men whom I had met with regularly for several decades. To be honest, if those friendships had not already been in place, I do not know where I would have turned or how I would have survived. How sad it is that so many people do not have those soul friends in place to hold them up when the storms come!

I am not proud of how I survived those impossible years. I am just thankful I survived. I lived with six and a half years of anxiety that crushed my heart. Now, I live daily with a different kind of pain, the pain of grief. I wish I could have trusted God more. I wish I could have been stronger and always held on firmly to the goodness of God. But the space I had cultivated over the many years before the storm gave me just enough strength for the day ahead. God continued through all those years to teach me. In very specific ways, He let me know that He was not abandoning me, even though at many times I did not feel close to Him. On more occasions than I can remember, I thanked God for the indispensable lessons about margin that became part of my DNA well before the storm.

[ ]

I dream now about standing on a beach where the waves lap at my feet as the sun rises over the horizon. Very few people are on the beach at such an early hour. As far as I can see, endless water and sky fill the landscape. I take a deep, effortless breath. The tension in my shoulders disappears. I know the joy of breathing.

One day, I will stand on that shore. Now, sadness mixes with hope. Grief accompanies each step now. We cannot rush grief. One day I know, because of the goodness of God, we will feel the sunshine again. We are seeing slivers of sunlight break through the clouds. Each month brings a little more healing.

I know that God will sustain us. "I remain confident of this: I will see the goodness of the LORD in the land of the living" (Ps. 27:13). I hear His encouragement: "Wait for the LORD; be strong and take heart and wait for the LORD" (v. 14). He says to me, "I will go before you and will level the mountains; I will break down gates of bronze and cut through bars of iron. I will give you hidden treasures, riches stored in secret places, so that you may know that I am the LORD, the God of Israel, who summons you by name." (Isa. 45:2–3).

[ ]

Almost thirty years after that night when I lay in bed, wondering whether I could survive the speeding train wreck that defined my life, I still struggle with times of overload. I take on too much at times and often am lured by that shiny new technology. I have come to realize that the core problem lies within me. Perhaps we can all agree with Pogo, the comic-strip character who said, "We have met the enemy, and he is us."

Deep in the center of my being, I have learned that life is not meant to be rushed and driven. God did not intend for us to be perpetually stressed. I have enjoyed green pastures and sat beside quiet waters. The journey of these thirty years, with its storms and blue skies, has taught me much about "the unforced rhythms of grace" that I believe God so passionately desires for us all to experience, even though I still have so much to learn.

BREATHING EXERCISE

Creating space to breathe is critical in the storms of life. Reflect on a storm in your life and the place that space did or did not play in helping you weather that storm.

Learning to Breathe Again

We have forgotten how to breathe. Well, not technically, not completely. We breathe; we just don't breathe well. The impact of poor breathing patterns affects every area of living. Dr. Andrew Weil, noted leader in the field of integrative medicine, asserts, "If I had to limit my advice on healthier living to just one tip, it would be simply to learn how to breathe correctly."[6]

Have you ever noticed how your breathing changes depending on the circumstances? When we are exhausted from a hectic schedule, we say we need to catch our breath. When we are nervous or anxious, our breathing becomes so shallow we wonder whether we are breathing at all. A primary symptom of a panic attack is shortness of breath. When we are fearful, we hardly breathe. When we are beginning to relax, without thinking, we find ourselves taking a nice, long, deep breath. What is telling to me is that even when nothing particularly stressful is going on with me, I realize I am still taking shallow breaths. Once I notice that, I also become aware of the tension building up in my shoulders.

Our breathing, for good and bad, parallels our living.

Breathing fascinates me. Belisa Vranich, author of *Breathe: The Simple, Revolutionary 14-Day Program to Improve Your Mental and Physical Health*, asserts that quality breathing is fundamental to healthy living. She touts that learning to breathe again can "lessen pain and help you heal faster; help your digestive problems, . . . lower your cortisol level, making for easier weight loss; and lower your blood pressure faster and more permanently than any medication on the market."[7] While breathing better may improve these problem areas, I cannot help but wonder whether she has the cart before the horse. Our faulty breathing is a consequence of our poor living, not the other way around.

She seems to acknowledge this later when she admits, "We want everything fast: We walk faster than we did ten years ago, we eat faster, we communicate faster, and we actually age faster when exposed to oxidative stress for too long a time. Acid reflux can even come from swallowing too fast, then jumping to the next task. We are under great pressure to go to sleep quickly and to wake up quickly. And, consequently what happens? Our breathing is constantly in 'fast mode,' shallow and quick, which in turn has terrible health repercussions."[8]

I remember a time long ago when breathing came easily for me. Two summers stand out. When I was about twelve, my summer was slow and simple. Long, unscheduled days blended into one another. Everyone in the neighborhood would ride bikes, play football, hang around until late afternoon. Each day at 4:00 p.m., we would all gather at the pool for ninety minutes of raucous play. Parents would rotate the duty of watching us to ensure no one was hurt. We played Sharks and Dolphins, and Marco Polo. We imitated Olympic divers, complete with parental judging. The most difficult decision each day was which game to play first. The whole summer, as I remember it, was carefree, stress-free, and full of joy.

A few summers later, when I was in high school, I taught swimming and tennis lessons with my brother, Mike. Each morning, we went out to a community pool in the country and taught a small group of beginners. None of them were training for Wimbledon. We were sort of glorified babysitters, with the luxury of a swimming pool and tennis courts at our disposal to keep everyone happy. After the morning "camp," Mike and I would drive to a nearby golf course and play eighteen holes of golf. We still laugh today about the summer of the "truncated dimples," named after the dimple pattern on the golf balls that we used to play. Our only stress was whether we could get in an extra nine holes each day.

I knew how to breathe in those days. Breathing came naturally. Joy was found in simplicity, the outdoors, and good fellowship. Those summers are gone. Happy-go-lucky afternoons are replaced by stress-filled weeks. And while responsibilities make carefree living seem unfathomable, Jesus didn't seem to think so. Living in tumultuous times of brutal oppression, He appealed to His disciples and to us that we need not worry. Our Father knows every hair on our heads. Jesus urged us to consider the lilies of the field and the birds of the air.

We need to learn to breathe again by learning to live again. Noise, speed, and overload are choking the life out of us. We have become so accustomed to our shallow breathing that we don't even notice it, much less understand the impact on our lives.

Life does not have to be this way! We desperately need to expose the sickness of overconsumption, overstimulation, and overscheduling. We need to understand our own part in creating these problems while at the same time addressing the external forces that seek to trap us in their addictive grasp. We need new eyes to see a better way to live—life according to "the unforced rhythms of grace," as Eugene Peterson put it in his translation of Jesus' words from Matthew 11:28–29 (THE MESSAGE).

Life with God.

Life interruptible by God.

Abundant life, with hundredfold fruitfulness.

We need to find the way to authentic, God-directed purpose, without the overwhelming stress, distraction, and corresponding hopelessness that life will never slow down.

It's not a coincidence that breathing freely takes me back to my childhood. Jesus called us to become like children (Matt. 18:3). Nor is it an accident that so many children and teenagers are suffering from unprecedented levels of anxiety and depression. Childhood has been lost, replaced by unrelenting distraction and the constant drive to achieve, whether academically, in sports, or by some other lure toward success.

We all need space to breathe again: children, teenagers, young adults, and older adults. Together, in the pages ahead, we will do soul-searching and hard work to create space in which we can breathe fresh, glorious, stress-free air.

I wish I could write this as one who has arrived, who has a clear formula that fits all scenarios. I cannot. I write as a fellow journeyman. I hope and believe that the lessons I have learned in the storms I have experienced will make your journey clearer and the walk more fruitful.

BREATHING EXERCISE

Reminisce about a time when you breathed freely; when life was light and joy was your companion. Write a paragraph and describe that time in as much detail as possible. Describe the circumstances and the feelings of that time. Take a deep breath and do your best to relive the experience. How does that make you feel? Nostalgic? Sad? Happy?

Key Takeaways

- Overload, like an out-of-control speeding train, feels like an impossible problem to address. Many people simply give up trying.
- Part of the problem is that busyness feeds our identity, our sense of importance. Busyness feeds our pride.
- Christians are often most susceptible to overload as they battle guilt over not doing enough, and an endless progression of intense needs.
- Jesus was neither rushed nor stressed. He calls us to a better way, living according to the "unforced rhythms of grace" (Matt. 11:28–29 THE MESSAGE).
- Our breathing mirrors our living.
- As we create space to breathe again, we will recover the peace and joy and purpose that God intends.

[2]
The Elephant Flying Under the Radar

God does not cease speaking, but the noise of the creatures without, and our passions within, deafens us, and stops our hearing.
We must silence every creature, we must silence ourselves, to
hear in the deep hush of the whole soul, the ineffable voice of the
spouse. We must bend the ear, because it is a gentle and delicate
voice, only heard by those who no longer hear anything else.

—François Fénelon

Naming the Elephant

When I think back on those days before I read *Margin*, I am
amazed at how blind I was. I guess my life did not look all
that different from everyone else's around me, so I never
questioned whether all of the good things I was doing could possibly be wrong. No one else was suggesting it either. I kept on running faster and faster, getting more exhausted, never thinking that
another way existed. My self-destructive path was seemingly the
price I had to pay to have "the abundant life." I felt guilty both that
I was not doing enough and that I was not strong enough to handle the pressure. I never considered that my "abundant life" was
really only a bloated life. My overloaded existence flew like a giant
elephant undetected beneath my radar and the radar of all around
me. In all those years leading up to my near crash, I never had a
single person suggest to me that I had too much on my plate. I was
blind to the elephant in the room, and so was everyone around

me. Life was not working well, but I was resigned to the belief that exhaustion was normal, and unavoidable.

I know now that a fundamental part of the problem is that I blamed the problem on the world around me. I thought "out there" was the issue, blind to the truth that the real issue lay within me.

Jesus addressed this clearly. "Are you still so dull? . . . Don't you see that whatever enters the mouth goes into the stomach and then out of the body? But the things that come out of a person's mouth come from the heart, and these defile them" (Matt. 15:16–18). The problem was my heart. My heart had created the place that invited overload and stress; the culture just willingly crashed the party.

What exactly is culture? Two metaphors come to mind. The first is of swimming in the ocean. When we swim out a bit, we find ourselves caught up in the current. We may not be able to feel the current unless it is very strong. We wouldn't even know we were in a current unless we looked in to the shore and saw how far we had drifted down the shoreline. Culture is like that current. We hardly feel its effect, because everyone else is floating with us, but when we view the shore, which does not move, we realize how far we have drifted.

The second metaphor is your local, neighborhood bar. Bars are fun, friendly places. Someone can choose to walk into a bar and have a glass of water, but he might feel a bit out of place. People generally feel more comfortable in bars if everyone else is drinking along with them. Culture is similar. We can live counterculturally, choosing solid boundaries on our schedules, consumption, and participation in technology. But like drinking only water at the bar, those choices will not make us popular. We may feel like an outcast if we choose not to be on the latest social media platform. Other parents may look askance if our children do not participate in the youth league that plays its games on Sundays. If you wait an hour or two to answer a text, you may be viewed as unresponsive, even rude. The list goes on and on, because culture influences every aspect of our lives. It influences careers, families, trends, churches, health. Like the bar, culture is not forcing us into a lifestyle of overload, but it makes the problem much more difficult to resist.

Just as in the ocean, if we swim over our heads in today's culture, we will have to fight the current. Like the water drinker at the neighborhood bar, we will need to address the peer pressure that culture exerts.

Alcoholics in recovery go through a rigorous process called the 12 Steps, step 4 of which is to do a thorough moral inventory. This inventory uncovers the internal workings and past residue that lead to outer, destructive practices. We will undergo a similar kind of inventory. We will address subconscious *fears* that show up in our behaviors and choices. We will examine *rationalizations* that we employ, our own internal loophole system that excuses us from change. And we will shine a light on *lies* that culture feeds us that, when consumed, make growth impossible. Then, armed with the truth, we will begin together the courageous process of recovering life and rediscovering joy.

I wish the whole process were not so difficult. I wish I could offer "ten easy steps to a stress-free life," but I can't. For substantive change to occur, our hearts need resetting. Ezekiel described it as "remov[ing] from you your heart of stone and giv[ing] you a heart of flesh" (Ezek. 36:26). I find it revealing that in the Bible, the root Greek root word for "saved" is the same as the word for "healed." If we want to be saved from this life-choking overload, then our hearts need to be healed. Healing comes from God, aided by our willing cooperation and participation.

BREATHING EXERCISE

Overload begins within us, and then is exacerbated by culture. What is your one nagging temptation that lures you to overload? Write down one antidote to that trap.

Our Fears

Fear is a great motivator. It can also stop us in our tracks. Psychologists suggest that the natural reaction to fear is either "fight" or "flight." This is true whether the fear is obvious (a lion is in our path) or subconscious. With obvious fears, we feel the adrenaline surge, the breath shorten, and anxiety build. Thrill seekers feed on fear, while for most people "phobias" are debilitating. Subconscious fears are no less harmful. Though we may hide subconscious fears behind more acceptable masks, they still alter our behavior. The difference is that we are less aware of why we are acting the way we are. In this sense we become like the apostle Paul, who wrote, "For what I want to do I do not do, but what I hate I do" (Rom. 7:15). Until we name the fear, we cannot address the root of our actions driven by the fear.

When it comes to the currents driving the cultural wave toward margin-less living, we will begin by addressing the fears attacking us from within.

We fear emptiness, so we fill every empty place.

Noise, hurry, angst, and constant action are antithetical to peace. Peace can be present alongside noise, but it cannot be cultivated in noise. Peace is learned. Peace is grown and allowed to mature. To the extent peace is already mature in a soul, it then continues to thrive even in the hostile environment of noise, activity, achievement, and drive. Absent rich quantities of the fertile environment of space, silence, and solitude, peace is like the seed sown in rocky soil, whose roots cannot grow deep. At first challenge, peace flitters away.

Space, silence, and solitude all presume emptiness. Space is by definition unoccupied. Silence is void of noise. Solitude is absence of other people. If we are afraid of being empty (without things, sound, and people), then we will unconsciously do whatever it takes to fill the emptiness.

I think of those precious days of summer that I described earlier. The other side of those days was the inevitable experience of boredom. Usually, by the afternoon of the first day of summer, I complained to my mom that I was bored. I had no idea what to do with the empty void created when school was out. The lack of structure made me itch. My mom would tell me, "Find something to do." Since she seemed unwilling to solve my horrible dilemma, I would eventually get up and get creative. The best days came out of the boredom, but not until I pushed through the discomfort.

As an adult, not much has changed. Boredom still is uncomfortable. I still resist it, fight it, and flee from it however I can. Shopping, busyness around the house, activities of any sort, thumbing through social media, all provide precious relief from the angst of emptiness. Only when we are willing to lean into the emptiness, to push through the awkwardness, do we find that peace and joy reside on the other side.

Cultivating an environment of space, silence, and solitude, though, is much like the process of getting into shape. Every time I have gone through that process—and there have been many times—I am sorely tempted to give up. The running and lifting are such a grind that I reevaluate the joys that come with being a little rotund, and I almost stop trying. Depending on how out of shape I am, eventually the exercise moves from grind to joy, and I begin to experience all of the additional benefits of being in shape.

At first, when we attempt to quiet down, the silence is loud and the solitude is lonely. We feel empty, and the emptiness scares us. It scares us because we wonder what lies beneath the surface of all our activity. Are we fundamentally empty people, insufficient on our own? Doubts creep in as to whether anything exists on the other side of the silence. We try to push through. A day, a week goes by, and we wonder whether we are wasting our time. We can easily conclude that we are not one of those types cut out for silence or solitude.

Press on! After not so very long, we move from painful to enjoyable to indispensable. We notice the inner silence influencing our work hours and our relationships. Too many people give up before they get to the sweetness.

We fear appearing worthless, so we compare ourselves to others.

Right beside our fear of emptiness is our fear of appearing worthless. *Worthless* is an interesting word. Tear it apart and it reads "worth less." Worth less than what? The very concept of being worthless implies comparison to something, someone, or some standard that is worth more. Once we begin the comparison game, we are on a never-ending carousel. No one wins. Someone is always richer, smarter, more beautiful, with a newer car, better-behaved children, and a deeper walk with God (or so it appears). In the rare case when we appear to measure up well, devilish pride lurks on the other side. This was the plight of the Pharisees. Comparison is a lose-lose proposition.

Nevertheless, comparison runs rampant. At an early age we learn to put on masks. The masks take a wide variety of forms: the language we use, the clothes we wear, the stuff we buy, the food we eat or don't eat, the music we play, the people with whom we hang out. Our culture has unspoken but well-defined ways of letting us know where we stand. Peer pressure is not only the temptation of teenagers. The chasm between who everyone wants us to be and who we believe ourselves to be on the inside is depressing. We manage that gap through carefully managing people's perceptions. We expose enough to be real, but not so much as to let people into the darker places. Social media exists, at least in part, to allow us to easily manage our image. Most everyone looks happy, well-liked, and interesting on social media.

Because our image is so important to us, we are forced to play the game. The game of keeping up an acceptable image takes time, emotions, and energy. While social media is the convenient punching bag as it relates to image, countless other ways of presenting an image exist. The cars we drive (be they fancy, showing how successful and cool we are, or modest, showing how humble we are) reflect a form of an image play. Posturing takes many forms and infuses everything we do.

Os Guinness writes about living for "the Audience of One." He teaches how the antidote to the insidious comparison trap is realizing that we answer only to God for the way we live. How freeing it would be to live my life with God's perspective as my driving motivation! I wouldn't need to impress people with how busy I am, my admirable accomplishments, or my extraordinary parenting prowess. I could live a life of contented, anonymous godliness.

My worth is solely connected to my identity as a beloved child of God. I become like the infant who takes all her cues from the reactions of her mother. How liberating to answer only to the Audience of One!

These fears speak to why change was so difficult for me many years ago, after I identified overload as my problem. Fears don't subside easily. New patterns are needed. Vigilance is required. Once we name the fears that underlie our harmful choices, we also have to call out the rationalizations (excuses) and the lies that keep us stuck in the melee of overload.

BREATHING EXERCISE

Write a paragraph about the place that fear plays in your overload. How do self-image, pride, and desire to please others feed the choices you make toward overload?

Our Rationalizations

Legend tells of a wise Indian chief known throughout the land for his insight and character. A reporter came to him one day, seeking to understand the source of his wisdom. The Indian chief answered, "I have two dogs telling me what to do. One sits on my right shoulder and tells me the right way. The other sits on my left shoulder and tells me the wrong way." He paused. The reporter anxiously asked, "Which one wins?" The Indian chief smiled and answered, "Well, of course, whichever one I feed the most."

Once I came to terms with the destruction overload wreaked in my life, I was in a quandary. I hated the negative effects of overload on me and my family but was addicted to the positive feelings of significance and achievement that accompanied each decision of excess. I had two dogs sitting on my shoulders. The overload dog sought to sway me through clever rationalizations designed to convince me that I didn't have a problem, that if I was diligent enough, I could have it all—the overload and the peace. By naming those rationalizations, I began to overcome the excuses, which, in reality, were thinly disguised lies. Here is my list of rationalizations:

It's not bad, so it must be okay.

As long as we can tell ourselves that the things we are doing are not bad, then we can comfortably move forward. We can buy more, schedule more, add more without a thought. "Not bad" becomes the standard. We reason that there is nothing wrong with buying the latest fashion or the newer car or the latest gadget. Nothing wrong with working a few more hours or taking on that additional church commitment. Nothing wrong with winding down with a few TV shows or stalking friends on Facebook. It's true. There is nothing wrong with any of these things. But just because none of these choices are bad doesn't mean that any of them are good. They may or may not be. When we expand our understanding of God's will to include anything as long as it is "not bad," then we are molding God into the image of the culture around us. With God, we do not decide what is "not bad"; we decide what is "His good."

If I were just better organized, I could do it all.

It's almost comical to realize the number of self-help books I have read on how to better keep myself organized and efficient. I have systems and techniques coming out my ears. None of them have helped me toward simplicity, because there is too much to organize. I have been kidding myself when I've allowed myself to think that if only I were a little more organized, then I wouldn't have to change my addiction to more. It's easier, though, to believe the lie than to change my beliefs and behavior.

I just need to prioritize better.

A cousin to the rationalization about being better organized is the one that suggests we just need to prioritize better. I laughed with a group that a recent list of my annual goals consisted of fourteen primary goals and thirty-one secondary goals. Needless to say, I was not successful in accomplishing all of my goals. No amount of hard work could have accomplished everything that I set out to do. Prioritizing wasn't the problem; quantity was the problem.

I just want my kids to have the best opportunities possible.

Our culture has become hyper-extreme when it comes to anything regarding our kids. We are considered bad parents if we deprive our kids of any opportunity to become all they can be. A full day of school and mountains of homework are not enough. So, we add in tutoring, music lessons, and traveling sports teams. We fill every spare moment of their lives, all in the name of opportunity. Meanwhile, our lives get filled along with theirs as we attend and manage their "opportunities." We can't stomach the thought that we might be the cause of our children becoming average.

The evidence does not suggest that our overall efforts are working. Kids are burning out in sports, academics, and life in general. Maybe not at first, but they, like us, cannot keep up the pace without eventually giving out. Our supposed good intentions are doing them and us no favors.

I know I'm exhausted, but it is not that bad.

It's hard to know if our exhaustion is "that bad" until we have experienced being rested. The goal of creating space is not to achieve nirvana, where we are always rested and energized. Such a state is not realistic and wouldn't be healthy anyway. We cannot always be perfectly balanced. Times come when we have to move fast and drive hard. Times should come when we also catch our breath and recoup. If it is hard to remember the last time you felt rested, then that suggests a problem. Jesus said, "Come to Me, all who are weary and heavy-laden, and I will give you rest" (Matt. 11:28 nasb). Clearly, He was suggesting that we should not always be exhausted.

It's just a stage.

This is one of those rationalizations that is particularly effective because it cannot be disproved, at least not until it is too late. The truth is that we go through stages when we have to go hard. The equal truth is that not every stage is meant to be overwhelming, nor are we meant to be perpetually overloaded. Every stage has the possibility to be lived within our physical, emotional, and financial means. It may not be easy, but it is possible.

There is nothing I can do about my schedule.

When all other excuses fail, throw up your hands and admit defeat. Often, because we are so worn-out, we don't even face how shallow this rationalization is. We can change! Our schedules can change. Our hearts can change. Our habits can change. Change may not be easy. We may choose not to change, but it will not be because we are incapable of change.

I'm not hurting anyone.

Actually, this is one of the most insidious rationalizations on the list, because the truth is, we are hurting everyone, including ourselves. Anxiety, depression, and suicide are on the rise. One would think, with all of the advantages of today's culture, we would be happier people, but evidence suggests otherwise. James Dobson wrote, "Crowded lives produce fatigue—and fatigue produces irritability—and irritability produces indifference—and indifference can be interpreted by the child as a lack of genuine affection and personal esteem."[1] We live in a hurting world, hungry to find a better way.

We step in the right direction when we admit our excuses. The solutions may not be apparent immediately, but when we shine a light on the truth, hope rears its head. Once hope enters the picture, overload loses some of its appeal.

BREATHING EXERCISE

Name the top two rationalizations that you use to justify overload. Write down the opposite truth that corresponds to the rationalization.

The Subtle Lies of Overload

We haven't just fallen into this margin-less, breathless life we are now living. Subtle forces have been at work, whispering to us, luring us to decisions and choices that have become the place we now find ourselves. I call these the Five Lies of Overload. Naming these lies, seeing them for what they are, and discerning their influence on our lives begins the process of changing the path that has been leading us to discontentment.

1. The Lie of Growing Proportions: "If a little bit is good, then more must be better, and a whole lot more must be the best."

I love to eat, and I have a massive sweet tooth that I am always trying to rein in. When I was a kid, I was proud of the fact that I never lost an eating contest with anyone, despite usually being much smaller than those against whom I competed. Once, as a young camper, I defeated a much-larger senior counselor after consuming more than a dozen slices of French toast. To be honest, I was still going strong, but he didn't "have the stomach for it." Another time, after I'd eaten a large buffet dinner, friends challenged me to eat a dozen Krispy Kreme doughnuts. Not a problem! Two nicknames for me around the house growing up were "Gut" and "Bottomless Pit."

The problem is that I love the taste of the food I am eating. From there, my mind rationally says, *If a little bit tastes good, then a whole lot will taste better, and a gluttonous amount will taste even better.* The logic sounds great. The consequences are disastrous. I can usually stuff myself without getting physically sick, but afterward I still pay the price. And then I have this problem of gaining weight. The list goes on.

The mentality of "more is better and a whole lot more is even better" creeps into so many areas of our lives without us even recognizing its allure. We think that it must always be better to earn more money. We think a newer car is always better than an older car. We think more exercise is better, more education is better, more ministry is better, more information is better, more gadgets are better, more dieting is better, more work is better, more free time is better, more vacation, more house, more dessert. You get the picture. "More" subtly becomes the force that drives our days, our decisions, our money, and our hearts. What is our alternative to more? Enough. The popular phrase thrown around these days that is rarely exercised is "less is more." The problem with this thinking is that more is still the desired end goal. We are simply trying to satisfy our insatiable hunger through a different means. The challenging truth is that "enough is enough."

Granted, times occur when "more" is needed. At times, we need more exercise or more prayer or more time. The issue is the indiscretion with which we apply the lie of more, such that it condones our tendency toward greed and gluttony, always justifying immediate gratification. Then, with "more" driving us, the necessary space to attend to the important is gone. With "more" driving us, wants trump needs.

2. The Lie of Significance: "I gain my significance from what I do and achieve, and from what those I am responsible for do and achieve."

Bob Buford wrote a fantastic book many years back called *Halftime: Moving from Success to Significance.* Moving people toward a life that is defined by something other than just making money is both admirable and valuable. The danger in this thinking, though, is the unspoken assumption that our significance or lack thereof is measured by what we do or do not do with our time on this earth. This can easily leave many people feeling as if they are wasting their lives or that their lives are somehow less than significant if they are not doing something that measures up on the significance status pole. Ministers and missionaries measure very high. Some CEOs and managers measure high depending on the companies they manage or run. Others, well, they may not rank very highly. Jobs that operate out of the limelight can wrongly leave people feeling insignificant and purposeless.

Our work does matter. Our gifts and talents are a great blessing to so many people. But the fruits of the Spirit are not salary, title, achievements, awards, recognition from others, and whether we drive a Mercedes (or Prius). In God's eyes, worth comes from Who made us. His attention goes first to what is in us, not what we do.

When our minds become focused on the significance of our lives, pressure mounts to continue to raise the bar. Even those with whom we associate, our family and friends, become reflections on our significance. Without ever realizing it, we take on more and more to feel better about ourselves and our worth, hoping also that others and God will feel better about us too. Saying no to good requests feels somehow selfish with this thinking.

This trap of trying to constantly measure up is exhausting. Trying to avoid letting down those who "need" us is relentless. We become an "overload tapeworm" that can never be satisfied. In my thirties, these constant requests to help fed my ego and pride. Since I was asked to help, I puffed up with the conceited thought that the church's mission depended on me. How gracious of me to bring my many and varied gifts to the rescue!

I look back on that time now and am embarrassed. God does not need me. He chooses out of His grace to invite me into the exciting things He is doing. He allows me to be a coworker. I hope I am a little less prone to feel indispensable these days, but I know that I am still so susceptible to trying to prove my worth to myself and to others. I hate to admit it, but I still love to impress people, particularly with my humility. Fortunately, God is gentle and patient with me.

These days I have learned to pause when I am asked to do something or lead something. After pausing, and often asking what others think who know me best, I am better able to discern what lies beneath my inclination to accept or reject the offer. When asked, I first create space, and in that space, often God whispers His thoughts.

3. The Lie of Need: "If I see a need and do not fill that need, I am a selfish, bad person."

My wise brother told me long ago, "The need does not dictate the call." Jesus operated by call. He never did anything that the Father did not tell Him to do. I often can't figure out how that worked for Him, because I do not hear the Father's voice that clearly. But the principle remains. God calls us to some things, not everything. I am not the Savior, Jesus is. I cannot save all the poor. I cannot save my kids. I cannot fix every problem. Not even close.

A fresh breeze of freedom comes with realizing that God is God and I am not. I relax and simply try to discern His voice. I now say no more often than I say yes. This extra space frees me up to enjoy the things I say yes to more, and not always rely on nonexistent reserves for energy. I now am more able to respond enthusiastically to the spontaneous opportunities that God often brings in my path.

Bruce Larson asks, "But is it possible that the most important thing that God has for me on any given day is not even on my agenda[?] Am I interruptible? Do I have time for the nonprogrammed things in my life? My response to those interruptions is the real test of my love."[2]

What a powerful, convicting question! Am I interruptible? Interruptible people are approachable people. Interruptible people are usually humble people without overinflated egos. When I am very busy, I get totally annoyed at interruptions, even ones from those I love dearly. When my life is too full, my body language communicates impatience. If we attempt to meet every need that comes our way, then we guarantee that we will not have the space to be interruptible.

As I often still struggle with the Lie of Need, it helps me to confess that I am more ego-driven than Spirit-driven. This is why I have such a need to create space. I have to pause to discern what is going on within me, to hear the still, small voice. If I act without pausing, I too often go in the wrong direction.

On the surface this may not seem like such a big deal since we are responding to a true need. This is the subtlety of the lie. This is where good is the enemy of the best. Our days are numbered. Our energy is limited. If we choose to meet needs without discretion, then we may miss the call we were meant to heed.

4. The Lie of "A Little Later": "I can postpone the important things of life, like relationships, exercise, and spiritual growth, and get to them a little later, when I am not so busy."

The important things in life rarely come to us with a blaring sense of urgency. Relationships don't fall apart without first being eroded. We don't gain ten pounds in a day. Our spiritual walk with God doesn't just disappear; it fades. Intervarsity Press put out a profound booklet several decades ago, when I was in college, called *The Tyranny of the Urgent*. It described this very lie. The urgent cries out, and the important moves to the back of the line. The important continues to quietly wait until it can wait no longer. Then a spouse leaves. A child disconnects. Depression settles in.

We cannot minimize the difficulty of resisting the demanding wails of the urgent. Some things have to be dealt with right away. But when we have built our lives in such a way that the urgent seems to be the only thing that we are ever doing, then we need to stop and think. Something needs to give . . . or something will break!

The urgent is best friends with busyness. I fall victim to the automatic response when asked, "How are you?"

"Really busy." I have even said that at times when I was not particularly busy.

As with those who struggle with the Lie of Need, the Lie of "A Little Later" feeds our egos. Those who live under the dictates of urgency feel incredibly important. When we are barraged with urgent tasks, we feel as if we are keeping the world (our world) from falling apart. What could be more important than saving the world from falling apart?

The Lie of "A Little Later" is called a lie because it is not true. It is a deception. Much of what we claim is urgent is not. If we could see the bigger picture, we would realize that the important is what is urgent. Tending to our children is urgent. Loving our spouses is urgent. Praying is urgent. Only by creating space in our lives will we have eyes to see what truly matters.

5. The Lie of Stimulation: "If I do not have constant stimulation, I may die."

Now we move to a whole new kind of lie affecting our time and our spirit. I could easily argue that this law should top the list of forces affecting our lack of space.

The confusing aspect of the Lie of Stimulation is that the pressure comes from both the inside and the outside. Sure, our culture has been overrun with stimulation from phones and music and games and information. But our internal drive to be stimulated is every bit as problematic. If it weren't, we could simply say no. No one seems to be able to consistently say no, myself included. I have tried so many "tricks," with varying degrees of success. The difficulty exposes that the issue is inside of me. I have forgotten how to be quiet and need to relearn quiet all over again. More than that, something inside of me fears the lack of stimulation. I have heard so many people describe how uncomfortable they are while driving without the radio on.

In the parable of the sower, Jesus described the seed that fell among thorns. When he interpreted the parable to His disciples, he said that the seed sown among thorns represents "those who hear the message, but all too quickly the message is crowded out by the cares and riches and pleasures of this life" (Luke 8:14 NLT). "Crowded out" is a good description of what constant stimulation does to our souls. Other translations use the word "choked." When a person is choked, she can't breathe. How desperately we need to learn to breathe again, and one of the fundamental issues is to release the chokehold that relentless stimulation has on us.

BREATHING EXERCISE

Which lie creates the most problems for you? Write down the opposite corresponding truth you need to claim.

Key Takeaways

The issue of overload is like an elephant flying under the radar. It often goes unnoticed and minimized, an inevitability that we can do nothing about.

- In order to make progress against the forces of overload, we must expose the fears, rationalizations, and lies which lure us into choices that continue to sabotage peace and joy.

- Our Fears
  - We fear emptiness, so we fill every empty place.
  - We fear appearing worthless, so we compare ourselves to others.
- Our Rationalizations
  - It's not bad, so it must be okay.
  - If I were just better organized, I could do it all.
  - I just need to prioritize better.
  - I just want my kids to have the best opportunities possible.
  - I know I'm exhausted, but it is not that bad.
  - It's just a stage.
  - There is nothing I can do about my schedule.
  - I'm not hurting anyone.
- The Subtle Lies of Overload
  - The Lie of Growing Proportions—"If a little bit is good, then more must be better, and a whole lot more must be the best."
  - The Lie of Significance—"I gain my significance from what I do and achieve, and from what those I am responsible for do and achieve."
  - The Lie of Need—"If I see a need and do not fill that need, I am a selfish, bad person."
  - The Lie of "A Little Later"—"I can postpone the important things of life, like relationships, exercise, and spiritual growth, and get to them a little later when I am not so busy."
  - The Lie of Stimulation—"If I do not have constant stimulation, I may die."

[3]
The Many Faces of Overload

In a culture where whirl is king, we must understand our emotional limits. Ulcers, migraines, nervous tension, and a dozen other symptoms mark our psychic overload. We are concerned not to live beyond our means financially; why do it emotionally?

—Richard Foster, *Freedom of Simplicity*

Overload affects us at every turn: hundreds of thousands of apps; news coming at us through email, radio, TV; gigantic grocery stores with insane numbers of choices, not to mention all of the organic and specialty stores that offer the one item that turns a single grocery run into two, three, or four grocery runs.

To address the pervasive nature of overload, we need to step back and admit the many ways it invades our lives. Otherwise, we are prone to address one area, think we are done, and miss the fifteen other ways in which we are inundated with too much.

As a way of looking at the problem, we are going to break the elephant "overload" into three broad categories, and then look at how those broad categories divide further into subcategories. As we do this, keep a mental scorecard of the degree of difficulty you personally have in each of these areas.

The three broad categories are *accumulation overload, opportunity overload,* and *distraction overload.* We will discuss them one at a time.

Accumulation Overload

Too Much to Buy

Shopping is the American way. Billions are spent to convince us that we need the latest thing, and that without the latest thing we will fall behind everyone else and be unhappy or unhealthy. For some, buying stuff borders on an addiction. For others, shopping is an activity to avoid boredom or to entertain themselves. Groceries, clothes, technology, sporting goods, crafts—almost everyone has at least one Achilles' heel. Mine is technology. I fall victim regularly to the glitzy new gadget that will make my life easier or perhaps make me seem cool. Looking around my desk as I write this, I see an Apple Watch, an iPhone, an iPad, a scanner, an Echo Dot, a printer, a label maker, a wireless charger, and a few other more incidental gadgets.

On the other side of the coin, we not only accumulate too much, we are reluctant to get rid of our possessions. Even when we have near duplicates, we rationalize that throwing away something we are still using is wasteful. Who knows? We might want to pass the item down to our kids. Plus, most people can think of no more odious task than clearing out junk. It exposes our gluttony with regard to things. The good news (not really!) is at least we are not alone. Almost everyone is overwhelmed with stuff (a polite word).

Too Many Choices

Part of accumulation overload is the choice overload lurking around the corner. As if I we don't struggle enough with overload, our culture baits us into even more accumulation. When we grocery shop for even the most basic product, such as a carton of milk, the options are mind-boggling. Fat-free, 1%, 2%, whole, lactose-free; dairy, soy, almond, coconut. The same can be said for every product we need. Recently, I went shopping for casual pants. I was overwhelmed by the different "fits" available.

I am a golfer. When I go in the new mega-stores now exclusively for golf (who would have thought fifty years ago that golf would have its own mega-store?), I can easily spend several hours oohing and aahing over the twenty different brands of irons; the fifty different drivers, each with its own shaft option; the one hundred–plus putters; the twenty or so brands of golf balls; and the dozen or so different choices of grips for my clubs.

Every different decision, from shopping to vacations to schools to restaurants, is accompanied by a ridiculous array of options. These options consume energy, time, and money. How are we supposed to simplify what we seemingly have no control over?

Too Much Debt (Too Little Savings)

One of the inevitable consequences of accumulation overload and constant advertising is that almost everyone except the most diligent or the wealthiest suffer stressful levels of financial debt. This debt becomes a snowball that affects health, relationships, and personal peace. It is telling that with all the many struggles that couples face, financial struggles are always near the top of the list of the causes of divorce. It doesn't have to be this way!

Too Much Clutter

My wife, Weezie, and I are currently in the process (it seems like a never-ending process) of trying to declutter our house. One of many problem areas is my closet. When I began years ago to tackle the accumulation overload in my life, I thought this small task of decluttering my closet would be one of the easier steps toward a clutter-free life. I thought, *Give that closet a solid thirty minutes to an hour; then move on to the next pile of mess.* I began with the clothes, and thirty minutes flew by like thirty seconds. I was exhausted from trying to make good decisions about what to throw away and what to keep, and after all that work, I couldn't even tell that I had been in the closet.

A few days later, I worked up the resolve and dove back into that closet. I culled another layer of clothes that, somehow, I'd missed the first time around, and then began working on the shelves. Am I this much of a slob?

Now, after four sessions of decluttering, working on my closet, which is not very big, progress is evident, but victory is far from secure. Soon, I will have to dive back in. Why? Partially, because of bad habits. Partially because of poor systems that create clutter. Partially because I still give in to the tendency to buy things I do not need but that others have told me I have to own. And partially because I hate cleaning out my closet.

If a simple closet is this difficult, how are we supposed to manage the rest of our lives? Not to be discouraging, but the task is huge. While we may never arrive at the blissful, perfect vision of a space-filled, balanced, productive, fruitful life, real progress and huge changes are possible.

BREATHING EXERCISE

On a scale of 1 to 10, how problematic is accumulation for you? What specific area creates the greatest temptation? What is one small step you can take to create balance in that area of temptation?

Opportunity Overload

Even if we are disciplined in the area of accumulation, overload picks a different door for its attack: opportunity overload. America has been nicknamed "the Land of Opportunity." Opportunity is great as long as we show the restraint to choose wisely among the thousands of choices that chip away at our time and our hearts. We need to transition from FOMO (Fear of Missing Out) to JOMO (Joy of Missing Out).

Let's parse that a little further. Much of what we fear missing isn't worth our time. We say yes out of fear that we might miss out on the fun (or the opportunity) and realize after the fact that there wasn't much to miss out on. One in four times we are glad we decided yes. The other times, we yawn. On the other hand, we underestimate the benefit of saying no. When we say a discriminating no, we create space for other joy and space for better opportunity. The discriminating no often creates the space for a more enthusiastic yes.

If we are able to make the difficult paradigm shift that balances FOMO and JOMO, we have the chance to experience the blessing of opportunity as opposed to the curse of overload. Opportunity overload shows itself in several different forms. Some of these affect everyone, while others enter in at a particular season of life.

Too Many Commitments

Everywhere we turn, we are asked to make another commitment. In isolation, one more volunteer request seems pretty innocuous, but all combined, the commitments cause schedule overload, which feed overload in other areas of our lives. From the moment we become adults, single or married, people are trying to get us to "sign up." If your life currently involves children, then the issue is more than multiplied. Moms particularly fall prey to this problem. The demands schools place on parents to attend every event and volunteer for every needless activity border on insanity. Unless we lead a hermit's life, the demands all around us to get involved threaten to swallow us.

Everything's a Competition

We joke in my family that we can't brush our teeth without turning it into a competition. I love competition and come from a family driven by winning, even if the other person doesn't know we are competing. My family is not alone, though. The competitive nature that permeates our culture feeds opportunity overload. Whether in our jobs, as parents, as a spouse, as an athlete, as one trying to improve oneself, the drive to be the best has become outrageous. Anything less than 110 percent (how does anyone do more than 100 percent?) is viewed with disdain, as accepting mediocrity. For parents, even if we accept this "mediocrity" personally, we are viewed as abusive if we hold our kids back from being the best they can be. Depriving a child of the remote possibility of being the next world soccer star by not signing him or her up for the elite travel soccer team is unthinkable. Every sport and every hobby has its extreme version. Being ordinary is unacceptable. Let me repeat that. In our culture, being ordinary is unacceptable. Since the truth is that we are all basically ordinary in the grand scheme of things, we are left feeling inadequate. The only option left is to try harder.

The Endless Degree

How can something as good as education be a source of overload? Perhaps as a by-product of our competitive culture, we give piles of homework in grade school, and exert relentless pressure on kids as early as ninth grade to watch their grades to so that they can beef up the college transcripts. In high school, we expect our kids to take multiple college-level courses to give them the best chance of getting into the best college. I thought taking college-level courses was the reason we went to college. This, of course, has placed an epidemic level of stress on our children, which, of course, leaps like a mosquito right onto the parents. A stressed-out family is an unhappy family.

For those early in the career journey, education is equally frustrating. A college degree is considered a starting point. Advanced degrees are only slightly better. Within the business world, the coveted MBA only slightly raises an eyebrow from potential employers. The education competition seems like a no-win game.

Spiritual One-Upmanship

Gordon MacDonald once quipped, "Why on one Sunday in five years when a New England snowstorm forced us to close down our church was it universally recognized as the most wonderful Lord's day they had ever had?"[1] Many churches mirror the overload of our culture. Staff are expected to outwork their lay counterparts out of passion and devotion. Volunteers are extended beyond reason, preferably accompanied by a pleasant smile. No judgment is intended here. We struggle in our churches to compete with a culture that offers exciting options, done with excellence. Certainly, we don't want to dishonor God with less than our best. But too often, the church has lost its countercultural voice. Add church commitments to already-overloaded schedules and Christians end up suffering the most from margin-less living.

Career Survival

Work overload used to be the primary source of overload. Futurists envisioned with the coming of the technological age that we would save so much time that workweeks would decrease to no more than twenty hours. The opposite has happened. Today, despite all the other inputs we have added into our lives outside of work, the average number of hours worked by the typical American continues to rise. For many people, work is not the main source of overload. But for more than a few people, work is still the first and foremost issue that needs to be addressed. Demands from bosses, never-ending work emails, the travel demands of the global economy, expectations of being available 24/7, and the need to please in order to get ahead make this a very difficult issue to address.

Opportunity overload reflects the complexity of combating the forces of culture. Simplistic answers will not suffice. In the end, if our daily schedules are overwhelming, whether by choice or by demand, then the dream of breathing again becomes just a fantasy. Whether the answer requires a Band-Aid, outpatient surgery, or radical open-heart surgery, if we hope to deal with the tyranny of overwhelm, opportunity overload must be addressed.

BREATHING EXERCISE

Where specifically does opportunity overload rear its head in your life? Name one small step toward balance that you can take in that area.

Distraction Overload

When Richard Swenson wrote *Margin* in 1992, email was in its infancy, as was the internet. Cell phones weighed twenty pounds, and the iPhone was not even a glimmer in Steve Jobs's eyes. Swenson wrote about the magnitude of the problem with overload, not even knowing the tsunami coming our way. Distraction overload now may be the worst offender of all the forms of overload. What distraction overload does is fill every potential gap, whether it is ten seconds or five minutes, with an appetizing temptation. Just this morning, as I prepared to write about distraction, while letting our dog out into the front yard, I pulled out my phone, ready to tap that beautiful square icon that beckoned my attention . . . and I paused. Not a day goes by that I do not still battle the temptation of distraction.

The psychic impact of lives without a spare second creates enormous issues. As we work to create space to breathe again, we will need to be brutally honest about our addiction to distraction. For now, here is a small sampling of the ways distraction screams its way into our every moment.

Information Avalanche

One of the more obvious areas of distraction overload is information. Information comes at us from everywhere, from our TVs, newspapers, magazines, apps, the internet, and radio. More information is available at our fingertips on every imaginable subject than has ever been available in the history of humanity. The moment anyone asks a question, and the answer is not immediately obvious, phones whip out like a six-shooter to see who can find the answer first. The ding of today's notifications has replaced the ring of yesteryear's telephone.

The information is not neutral, either. Terrible stories of tragedy, vicious political commentary, and fear-inducing warnings dominate. We know we have to manage the sources and streams of information simply to keep from going crazy, but few of us have intentional strategies that put reasonable boundaries on the bombardment.

Technology Obsession

I love technology! I am awed by what can be done today through technology. Devices now, through a sensor worn on a wrist-watch-like device, track how many calories we consume and analyze our sleep cycles. Sad to say, I always want to be the first to see what is out there. It's fun to me. And technology dramatically improves life from many perspectives. But technology has lodged itself too deep in too many people's hearts. In a recent study where teens were asked to abstain from all technology for twenty-four hours, the responses were more than a little disturbing:

- "I began going crazy."
- "I felt paralyzed—almost handicapped in my ability to live."
- "I felt dead."
- "Emptiness. Emptiness overwhelms me."
- "Unplugging . . . felt like turning off a life-support system."
- "I sat in my bed and stared blankly. I had nothing to do."
- "The feeling of nothing passed into my heart . . . I felt like I had lost something important."

We are kidding ourselves if we think that we can address the overload in our lives without also addressing the place that technology has come to occupy in our lives. If you are among the few for whom technology is in check, then continue to enjoy its benefits in balance. For the rest of us, we need to decide how radical our solutions will need to be. Knowing that the challenges will only escalate with time, now is the best opportunity to step back and choose our path. More to come on this!

Bottom Line

The variables we just discussed conspire to overwhelm us all day, every day. Depending on your personality, upbringing, finances, and habits, certain areas will be worse problems than others.

Perhaps the most insidious aspect of this overload is what it precludes in our lives. We are not only overloaded in multiple arenas, but we are also drastically underloaded in so many other areas that desperately need our attention.

What happens to many people who begin to deal with their overloaded lives is that once they have emptied themselves of the destructive parts (even good things can be destructive in large quantities), they simply feel empty because they do not fill part of that void with healthier choices. The emptiness feels worse than the overload, so they quickly revert back to the less-painful overload.

Life is more than avoiding bad things. "Do not" will only take us so far. We also have the chance to build a new life filled with the richest fare that our broken world has to offer. Our hope is not only to eliminate the overload and overwhelm leaving us in a neutral average, but to experience abundance in balance, purposeful work with luxurious rest, and intimate relationship with God and others that satisfies the soul.

BREATHING EXERCISE

Which area of overload—accumulation, opportunity, or distraction—is most difficult for you to overcome? Write about its place in your life in detail. Identify a friend who shares the problem, and meet to develop a plan together to make progress.

Key Takeaways

- Overload attacks us from all sides. If we hope to address the destructive effects of overload, we will need to face the breadth of its impact in our lives.
- There are three broad categories of overload: *accumulation overload, opportunity overload,* and *distraction overload.*
- Accumulation Overload
  - Too Much to Buy: Shopping is America's new pastime.
  - Too Many Choices: We now have a hundred options for every choice.
  - Too Much Debt: Accumulation creates debt and financial pressures.
  - Too Much Clutter: Accumulation creates clutter, which exacerbates overload.
- Opportunity Overload
  - Too many commitments: Everywhere we turn we are asked to make another commitment.
  - Everything's a Competition: The drive to be the best at all costs creates relentless pressure.
  - The Endless Degree: Education, from grade school through adulthood, has become a new source of overload.
  - Spiritual One-Upmanship: Churches have often bought into the extreme pursuit of excellence, trying to keep up with secular culture.

- Career Survival: What used to be the prime source of overload, career, is now one of many issues. Still, the demands of career create major hurdles for many people who are fighting overload.
- Distraction Overload
  - Information Avalanche: The dual problem of information overload is both the quantity and the emotional exhaustion that accompanies the nonstop stream of information.
  - Technology Obsession: Technology has a Jekyll/Hyde quality, offering immense benefits and consuming issues.
- We address overload, not just to remove the unhealthy, but to make room for the abundant life that God has for us, a life of balance, purpose, rest, and relationship.

[P A R T   T W O]

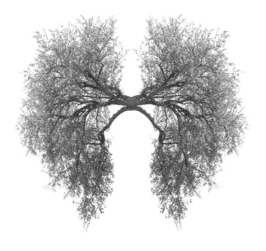

Hope Through Renovation

[4]

Demolition and Renovation

It would seem that Our Lord finds our desires not too strong, but too weak. We are half-hearted creatures, fooling around with drink and sex and ambition when infinite joy is offered us, like an ignorant child who wants to go on making mud pies in a slum because he cannot imagine what is meant by the offer of a holiday at the sea. We are far too easily pleased.

C. S. Lewis, *The Weight of Glory*[1]

The Work of Renovation

A few years ago, we undertook the horrendous project of renovating our kitchen. Our kitchen had not been touched since we first built our house more than twenty years ago. We loved the kitchen then, but time took its inevitable toll, and the once-great bastion of food and family looked dated, with appliances that no longer worked, and drawers crammed with junk dating back to the early days of our children. When, finally, our oven started only working sporadically, we knew the time had come. Knowing this major project was on the horizon, we had saved for this inevitable day. And so, we decided to bite the bullet.

Our first step was the plan. One option was to put a Band-Aid on this mammoth project by only replacing a few appliances and fixing a few cabinets. The Band-Aid would mean much less disruption and a fraction of the budget. But in the end, we knew we would be frustrated with a halfway solution. Besides, we had carefully saved for this most-glaring eyesore. A full renovation was in store. We engaged the help of a designer, who came up with a detailed plan that excited us. The vision of a fresh, inviting space thrilled us. It was time to get to work!

In a matter of days, our entire house was turned upside down. The dining room housed all of our pantry items, pots and pans, plates, and other miscellaneous paraphernalia; kitchen table, chairs, and stools stacked up in our family room. Every living space on our first floor was jammed full of kitchen odds and ends. Our basement was filled with new appliances that were awaiting the appointed time. Alongside the yet-to-be-installed appliances were the old appliances awaiting our decision as to whether we would sell them, give them to our local thrift store, or throw them away. The upstairs was the only place that was relatively unscathed by our simple kitchen renovation.

Then the demolition began. Dust everywhere. Ear-shattering noise, as we pulled up the tile floor and ripped off the countertop. Our once-beautiful kitchen that was tired and dysfunctional now looked as if a bomb had gone off in it. No matter how much we tried to be realistic about the disruption we were choosing to undergo in this renovation, the reality was much worse.

Slowly, very slowly, we moved from total demolition to renovation. New floors were laid. New appliances were installed. Countertops were next, then cabinet work. We painted the entire kitchen a fresh color and bought cool stools to complement our new granite countertop. While the construction crew did their magic, we cleared out every drawer and pared down our pantry to the few items we use regularly. Even though the whole process took only about three months, it seemed like twice that. Now we have a brand-new, fully decluttered, bright, pristine kitchen. We cook more and entertain more in our newly renovated kitchen. One could argue that not much has actually changed. We have basically the same appliances and the same amount of space, yet our entire experience is different now. We tolerated our kitchen before. We love our kitchen now!

[   ]

Renovation is not for the faint of heart. It takes a high level of commitment and careful forethought. The end results, though, will be life changing.

These are the steps we took with our kitchen: *plan, demolish*, then *renovate*. Beginning the project without a plan would have been idiocy. Equally, it would have been silly to think of renovating before we had demolished the old junk that no longer was working. Often, this is exactly what we try to do with our lives. We try to add on good things without getting rid of the bad things that don't work or serve us any longer.

When it comes to our daily lives, demolition of old ways may feel like turning around the *Titanic*. A lifetime of patterns is deeply ingrained. In some sense, these patterns work for us, even if we are frustrated at where they have brought us. We are comfortable in our discontentment, as long as we don't have to risk change. Change is painful and unpredictable. Demolition is both about facing the overwhelming accumulation that clutters our lives and addressing unhealthy patterns that develop through the years.

As we look at the demolition of old ways of frantic living, filled with stress, we will look at our patterns. Changing patterns will initially be uncomfortable. Change always is. For most of us, the benefits will bring immediate rewards. Even with those immediate rewards, sticking with the changes will be a challenge. The long-term rewards will be for those who commit to push through the resistance to change.

We will also look at the breadth of renovation. When we renovated our kitchen, we considered only replacing the appliances. The appliances were the most problematic issue. Had we done that, we would have gained a functional kitchen again. We could have cooked meals but would have been constantly frustrated at cabinet doors with sprung hinges. The paint and the tile, more than twenty years old, took the spark out of being in the kitchen. Had we only replaced the appliances, we would still be dissatisfied, only enjoying a fraction of the benefit we now love so much.

There's a lesson to be learned there. The reason so many people do not undertake personal renovation is that it is such a huge job. I am going to work to make that huge job more manageable for you by breaking it down into bite-sized chunks.

We will begin by establishing a plan. We are going to take a personal inventory of the personal renovation work we need to do. Much as we broke our kitchen renovation into categories—appliances, flooring, countertops, cabinetry, painting, and decorating—we will delve into all of the specific categories that might need revamping in our lives.

Once we get rid of the old, worn-out crud, we will replace the old, dysfunctional ways. What new "appliances," "countertops," and "cabinets" will make all this hard work worthwhile? Finally, we are going to give attention to a beautiful, spacious, purposeful vision for our future. The renovated life will barely resemble the previous, frenetic life. When I used to walk in our kitchen, my shoulders would sag with all of the work to be done. Now, I physically feel myself taking a deep breath. I feel invitation and possibility in a place that used to drain energy. This is the hope for those who are overloaded and overwhelmed.

BREATHING EXERCISE

Describe a renovation that you experienced. What was the space like before the renovation? What was the experience of demolition? How did the space change after the renovation was completed? What area of your life is most in need of renovation?

Assessing the Job

For some people, a renovation is nothing more than a sprucing up. Everything may be in working order but feel old and unexciting. Routines have become ruts. Patterns in relationships have become stale. For others, renovation requires a total gutting. Regardless of where you are personally, the starting point is an honest assessment of the work ahead. This is where you come in and do more than read pages. I want to ask you to assess your life.

Here is a Life Renovation Assessment link that will allow you to think through what is ahead (www.SpaceToBreatheAgain.com). You can do this work on your own in a private, nonthreatening way.

Here is a preview of the assessment tool.

For each of eight areas, I will ask you to rank your health on a scale of 1 to 10, with 1 meaning you are in horrible shape and in need of drastic help, and 10 meaning you have this area nailed and can't think of anything you need to improve.

Then, for each of the areas, I will ask you to write out a brief "State of the Union" report on how you are currently doing in that area—something more than one sentence and less than a book. The value comes as you take your time with this exercise and give focused thought to this SOTU report.

When you finish this exercise, you will have a complete personal assessment of where you are right now. If you want to be brave, then you can ask a spouse or a close friend to fill out an assessment on his or her perception of where you are in each of these areas. The reality is we all have blind spots that we cannot see. Bringing a few people into our assessment only adds value and enhances clarity.

The tendency will be to think that you do not need to take this assessment, that you know how you are doing. As I have shared this assessment with many people, I have been amazed by how often people come back surprised by their results. I hear comments like, "I had no idea how bad things had become," or "I can see clearly now where I need some real work." The process is simple, but the insights may be arresting. Give it a try!

Here are the categories we will examine:

- **Time.** Our lives are composed of minutes, days, weeks, months, and years. How well do we manage our time, our schedules, our commitments? Are we constantly rushing, out of breath, busy to the point of frustration and exhaustion? Recognizing the demands others place on our time, whether from jobs, friends, or family, we are still ultimately responsible for how we live each minute. Any renovation will need to take seriously the broken habits and patterns with time. How are we doing in that area?

- **Spaces.** The space in which we live and work has a major effect on our emotions and our spirits. Are our spaces life-giving? Are they cluttered? Do they consume too much energy as we try to maintain perfect orderliness? Are they helping us live better, more enjoyable lives, or are they a source of constant frustration and endless upkeep?

- **Technology.** Is technology a tool, a distraction, or an addiction? Is its place in our lives appropriate, or overwhelming? Does it serve who we want to become, or distort who we are becoming?

- **Noise.** Noise comes at us through our eyes and our ears. For many of us, stimulation is so unrelenting that we have no possibility of finding peace. God's whisper is lost in the screaming voices vying for our attention. Is there any place of quiet where peace can reside and grow?

- **Finances.** Everyone, even the wealthiest, have to deal with the place that money plays in life. For some, accumulated debt strangles joy and tests relationships. For others, sticking to a budget or wrangling out-of-control spending is the problem. A few have plenty of money, but cannot stop thinking about it, worrying if enough is enough. Are you saving?

Are you giving generously? Are you living within your means with a plan? Are money issues so consuming that they dominate more important areas?

- **Relationships.** Joy and heartache flow from our relationships. Our emotions are drained or uplifted by the people around us. Are we lonely? Do we have good friends with whom we can share our struggles and hopes? Is a toxic relationship dragging us to dark places?

- **Faith.** Where are you in your relationship with God? Are you growing or have you stagnated, or even worse, fallen away from faith? Do you miss that "first love" that you once had for God?

- **Personal Growth.** Are you investing in yourself? Are you reading? Are you exercising? Are you growing into the person you one day aspire to become?

You can see that there is a lot to think about here. Without a doubt, these silos that we are assessing bleed into one another. Every area affects every other area. The hope in this assessment is to see the breadth of the work we have ahead of us and to understand better the primary sources of our struggles.

Once we are finished assessing our overall health, where we are right now, we can tackle the work of renovating these areas, and then enjoy a fresh new way of living and breathing. We will address some of the areas directly, particularly as they impact our ability to create space. We will work on other areas indirectly. Armed with our honest assessment, we will center on where we most need the help.

When I take a trip, three pieces of information are critical. First, I need to know my destination. Am I going to California or to New York? No point in starting the car without knowing where you are headed. Second, I need to know where I am starting the trip. The route to California is quite different leaving from Chicago than from Richmond, where I live. On a trip, the starting point is usually pretty obvious. Not so when we are talking about the complexities of our lives. This is the purpose of the Life Renovation Assessment. Finally, once we know where we are headed and from where we will start, we choose the path. Will I take the interstate or the back roads? Will I drive through the night or take a leisurely trip? Once we are clear on the starting point, where we individually are beginning our journey, then we will shift to our desired destination and the path to that destination.

A few years back, I made a cross-country road trip in a U-Haul truck with my son Chris. Each day we drove twelve to sixteen hours, trying to get home in the quickest time possible. I often live my life that way—driven—missing all the magnificent scenery along the way.

In our whole-life renovation that we will undertake, I hope we won't do that. There is joy in the journey. And though the journey may be challenging, the views along the way will be breathtaking.

BREATHING EXERCISE

Take the Life Renovation Assessment. Celebrate your healthiness. Identify what most needs renovation.

The "Renovator's Toolbox"

Before we move into the process of renovating the various areas of our lives, I want to offer particular strategies that will help us approach each of these challenges. I think of these as our *renovator's toolbox*. A contractor would never think of beginning a renovation without a full set of tools perfectly designed for the tasks that lie ahead. Sometimes a hammer is needed, other times a wrench. As we attack the challenge of personal renovation, we need a full toolbox of strategies to attack the project. This section will offer those tools.

I am aware that using a word such as "attack" seems counterproductive to the goal of learning to breathe again. Breathing again implies being in a relaxed state, not on high alert. But before we get to that relaxed place, we must address the war raging within us and all around us. Vigilance comes first; rest is the reward. In this section, we will lay out various tools, and then look at particular areas where these tools might come in handy. We will then refer back to these tools when we dive into the rubble that needs renovating. A few strategies will show up throughout the pages ahead. They are paradigms of change that can be applied in a wide variety of situations. Here are five specific tools for your renovator's toolbox:

Tool #1: Dominoes

The problem of overloaded living is multitiered. We don't just have one problem with too much; we have many problem areas of excess. Despite this, often, one major overload monster feeds all the other monsters. Consider the family for whom financial margin is the major villain. The fallout of financial overload is anxiety, relational stress, excess accumulation, clutter, and a need to work long hours to pay the bills. If the first domino of financial overload topples, many other dominoes fall right behind it.

Or consider the area of technology overload. Addressing this area impacts relational stress, financial stress (technology costs money), sleep stress, and priority stress. Overload is always a game of dominoes. Is there an obvious first domino you need to attack? Your Life Renovation Assessment may help you answer these questions.

The tool of playing dominoes works on two levels. If we are able to identify one major area of struggle that is disrupting all the other areas, then we know where to better focus our attention. Playing dominoes with overload also works on the micro level.

Small bad habits create monster problems. C. S. Lewis captured this threat perfectly in his ingenious book *The Screwtape Letters*. In it, a senior demon writes to a junior demon, "It does not matter how small the sins are provided that their cumulative effect is to edge the man away from the Light and out into the Nothing. Murder is no better than cards if cards can do the trick. Indeed the safest road to Hell is the gradual one—the gentle slope, soft underfoot, without sudden turnings, without milestones, without signposts."[2] As usual, I found this out the hard way.

Long after I began my quest to find margin in my life, attack launched from the rear. It came in the form of *Words with Friends*, an innocuous, Scrabble-like electronic game played on a phone or a tablet. Somewhere—on Facebook, I think—someone challenged me to a friendly game. I never turn down a challenge or competition, so I accepted . . . and accepted . . . and accepted. In no time, I had multiple games going on with a cadre of friends. I was pretty good at the game (in my humble opinion), so each time, I felt a rush when I won. I began squeezing games in all the small, empty spaces of each day. I would make a move during a bathroom break, between meetings, and even during meetings if I could get away with it. At night, instead of reading, I amused myself with a game or two or three. On more than one night, I stayed up to the wee hours playing someone equally addicted to the game.

All this time, I still did my job, took care of things at home, and had my quiet times, although I have to admit that I caught up on any outstanding moves before I picked up my Bible. I was constantly distracted. No room existed for anything positive, because it was all filled with *Words with Friends*. Others, including my wife and kids, commented in a nice way about my obsession. I defended myself by saying something to the effect that I wasn't hurting anybody.

Finally, I realized that the obsession was out of hand. I knew myself well enough to know that moderation was not an option. In one grand gesture, I let everyone know that I was taking a hiatus from the game. In my own mind, I knew I could never return. I went cold turkey. I had classic withdrawal symptoms as I deleted the app from all my devices. Then, I felt the chains fall off and freedom return to me. I remembered what space felt like. I learned all over again what it felt like to breathe again.

Silly as it seems, for many of us the small things are the most egregious sources of overload. We may not lead crazy-busy lives, but we have perpetual angst and stress because there is no space to catch our breath. This rears its head throughout our minutes and hours. We end days exhausted, yet unable to point to what we accomplished. Some people may have one weak spot that is the constant budget buster, or one food that derails them every time they try to lose weight. The smartphone may be a constant interruption, keeping us distracted. How do we make real progress with these small problems?

Is there a lead domino that is triggering overload for you? Overturning that domino may unleash a whole new freedom that will be the first step to breathing again.

Tool #2: Systems

For years, I struggled with the tedious task of filing papers. Each week, piles of papers, most of them bills, stacked up in my in-box at home. As distasteful as it was to pay those bills, filing them was even more odious. So, the paid bills would stack up, cluttering my office, until once or twice a year I reluctantly tackled the task of putting each bill in its proper place.

One day, a friend suggested, "Just stop it."

"How do I do that?" I asked.

He explained that, in reality, we rarely ever go back and look at those bills. Most of them can be found online anyway. Further, he recommended that if I insisted on keeping paper copies, I keep them all in one folder, labeled by year with the simple title "20__ Bills." With that one suggestion, I was able to take a distasteful task that I hated doing and eliminate it. Now, I pay the bills, grab the whole stack, and stuff them in the one folder. In the several years since implementing this system, I have never been unable to locate a previously paid bill. Great systems are game changers!

Let's dig into this further!

One of the most overrated character traits is willpower. Yet, we blame much of our inability to make progress on willpower. What if you could change a problematic habit with absolutely no will- power? Let me use an extreme example. If for some strange reason I thought that listening to the radio in my car was a huge problem for me, how might I go about addressing the problem? I might post an index card above my radio, telling me not to touch the radio. That could help a little, but I still need willpower to obey the card. Instead, what if I went to the dealership and had them remove the radio altogether. While extreme, that would solve the problem. I no longer need willpower. I have automated my success. Or consider a struggle that many us face: an addictive obsession with some form of social media. I might try to resist the urge to pull up my favorite app at every spare moment, and I will probably fail. I could move it to the back page on my phone, and that might encourage me to be strong, but I am still likely to fall prey to the temptation. Another possibility is that I can delete the app from all devices. Since reload- ing the app is a pain, I am giving my willpower a huge boost. If the app is not on my phone, I have to go to a web browser to feed my hunger. Of course, the ultimate answer is to delete the social media account altogether. Georgetown associate professor Cal Newport suggests this strategy in *Digital Minimalism*.[3] He challenges his read- ers to delete all digital temptations for thirty days, and then carefully, reluctantly, reengage with the enticement once they have broken the addictive lure.

When we make success automatic through systems, we increase our chances of success exponentially. Despite all our efforts, we will still need at least a small dose of willpower and discipline. Willpower and creativity are needed to make the initial hard steps to set up the system, and some discipline is required to keep us from undoing sys- tems we have set up. Even so, a well-designed system is nine-tenths of the battle.

Systems have a dual benefit. A good system saves us time because something is automatic that we used to do manually. We might use systems to automate areas of our lives that regularly trip us up, such as forgetting appointments or building habits. Creating a system is simply a means to take an area that we struggle with regularly and implement a process that ensures the result we want. A very simple example is setting up our mortgage for automatic payment with the bank to make certain that it is never late. Systems come in all varieties and colors. The balance is to have the right systems in place to help us without creating undesired rigidity. Systems should be designed to free us up and keep us pointed in the right direction.

Two of the most effective applications of systems for me are repeating tasks and blocking calendar events. Personally, I use a digital task manager called *Things* to help me. It enables me to set up repeating tasks at whatever interval I want, whether daily, weekly, or monthly, to help remind me and nudge me. I use repeating tasks daily to help me regarding habits I am trying to develop. I also use repeating tasks weekly to ensure I am reviewing my goals, planning my week, checking my budget, and so on.

Another system I use is time blocking, which is setting aside chunks of time in a calendar to point my time in the direction of my priorities. Each week I block large chunks of time in my calendar for exercise, writing, and reading to make sure that my week is moving toward my goals and priorities.

A key to thinking about systems is to realize that we struggle not because we are weak or bad but because we have not done the front-end work of setting up a system to give us the boost we need to succeed. Without a system, we are relegated to amassing sufficient willpower over and over again. What an exhausting way to live!

In the appendix, I have listed several areas and questions related to possible systems. These systems are by no means all-encompassing, nor are they ones that everyone will need or want to embrace. You may want to highlight one or two that could work for you. They are intended to provoke thoughts and creative solutions that might work for you. I hope they are helpful!

Tool #3: Fasting

It may seem old-fashioned, or we may think that fasting is just something from the Old Testament, but fasting is a practice that we can use effectively and broadly to effect change in any area of our lives. The concept is simple. Consider any area of life where you are prone to excess, out-of-control behavior. Fasting means to cut that behavior off completely for a prescribed period of time. The amount of time may be adjusted based on the severity of the need. Several biblical examples exist. The most obvious is the fast from food. Jesus fasted for forty days and then said, "Man shall not live by bread alone" (Matt. 4:4 NKJV). Periodic fasting from food, whether for a meal, a day, or longer, helps break the hold that food has on us. Fasting can be used to help us in any area of life. We might fast from shopping or fast from TV. We might fast from alcohol or social media. When we do without, we are asserting that we are able to do without. This, by itself, is empowering and freeing.

Another form of fasting is counterbalancing an undesirable behavior with the opposite behavior. Tithing fits this description. Since we are a money-hungry culture, the antidote to money worship is tithing, which in the Bible refers to giving away the first tenth of everything we make. By practicing tithing, we are proclaiming that money does not own us. We are free not to hoard. We are free not to spend. We are free to give. This practice, particularly when exercised over a period of years, begins to free our hearts from the seduction of accumulation.

We can apply this principle of doing without to so many areas of our lives.

- Technology: Fast from your phone or from an app. As a potential antidote, read only physical books before bedtime.
- Noise: Fast from the radio, from podcasts, from earphones.
- TV: Fast from channel surfing and/or binge-watching. Fast from TV for one day per week.

- Food: Fast one meal or a specific food, perhaps sweets or breads.
- Alcohol: Fast from drinking when out with friends or when you are at home. Or pick a night to abstain.
- Shopping: Fast from shopping as a stress reducer, from online shopping, or from a particular category (clothes, technology, etc.).
- Social media: Take your pick! Fast for one or two days. Fast from a particular app.
- Internet browsing: Stay off the internet after 8:00 p.m. (you can use apps such as Screen Time and Freedom to help).
- Fast from your phone before you spend time with God.

Be bold. What is the worst that can happen? Fasting in any one of these areas for a period of time will be revolutionary. If nothing else, strategic fasting breaks the hold that various issues have in our lives. Fasting helps us appreciate what we miss. It puts things into perspective.

A final word. One of the rages these days in dieting is intermittent fasting. This is fasting for sixteen to eighteen hours of a twenty-four-hour day. This "hack," which has had tremendous results for those who want to lose weight, can be applied to many areas of overload that we want to control. Perhaps we try an intermittent fast of four hours from our phones. Or we try a one-trip fast from the radio or music while traveling. If we are honest about our struggles and creative about our solutions, we can chip away at the addictiveness of overload.

Tool #4: Firewall

Some areas that are out of control in our lives cannot be solved by quick hacks. These problems are more systemic and require major, life-altering work. In these cases, I suggest building a firewall.

When large forest fires are out of control, experienced firefighters know that they cannot fight these fires head-on. Pouring water directly on those kinds of flames will cause them to get worse. Instead, they build a firewall. They move some safe distance in front of the wall of flame and build a deep trench the length of the fire and fill it with water. When the fire reaches the trench and there is nothing to sustain the fire, it dies out.

This tool can be used in more extreme cases of overload. When I was first learning about the concepts of margin, my life was so overloaded that it seemed impossible to make a dent. After discarding the low-hanging fruit of excess, I felt the tiniest twinge of relief, but was frustrated at how hard the whole process was becoming. The fix was much more complicated than employing a few minor hacks. So, I began to build a firewall.

The worst offender for me at the time was my schedule. Running four small businesses, serving as an elder, teaching a Sunday school class, leading a search committee for a new pastor, and trying to be a good husband and father, raising three small children, was more than was humanly possible. On the surface it did not seem as if there was anything to give up. This was where the firewall came in. I made several specific choices. I looked at each volunteer commitment. If possible, without being irresponsible, I backed out of the commitment. If it was not possible, I noted the end date of that commitment (the firewall) on my calendar and internally committed to stop the activity and not replace it with anything else, no matter how appealing. My calendar didn't look very different for the next month or two, but after that, I could see a few days and weeks that almost seemed normal. As soon as I did this, I finally had space to breathe again. I was still overloaded to the extreme, but I could see a light at the end of the tunnel. That light was a firewall. I knew if I could just hang in there for a little bit longer, relief was coming.

On top of this, I committed to practicing the Sabbath. I was convinced that the Sabbath was a command from God for my own good. Even though taking a twenty-four-hour break from checking things off my list did not seem possible at the time, I considered it a matter of obedience, so I did it. I remember distinctly how, for the first month or so of Sabbaths, Weezie and I would take turns taking long naps while the other one played with the kids. We had no energy to enjoy the day as it was intended because we were so exhausted going into it. So, we just rested. This also gave me hope because I realized that no matter how crazy or bad any particular week was, Sunday was coming. Rest was right around the corner. Sunday became my mini firewall at the end of overwhelming weeks. The combination of knowing that short-term relief was always close by and longer-term relief would eventually come, allowed me to get through a very difficult period.

My situation may not have any parallels to your situation. The deeper the hole, the more desperate the feeling. But once we face the problem, then we can apply creative solutions, some of which may take a long time to fully implement, and begin to experience blessed relief.

Tool #5: Boundaries

Moderation comes more easily to some people. I am not one of those people. I am wired for excess. A little bit more always seems better to me. But as I have said already, too much is always too much. Therefore, I self-impose boundaries throughout my life. We implemented this strategy when the children were young. We limited the major extracurricular activities that each one did to a single pursuit. They could play youth league basketball, but not basketball and volleyball. We chose to say no to travel sports. These were very hard, unpopular decisions in our household, but ones that we never regretted. We put boundaries on video games and TV. In our own lives, we put boundaries on the number of nights out each week and the number of volunteer commitments. Almost any area, in business or personally, at home or outside of the home, is ripe for implementing boundaries.

Boundaries are best when they are specific. "Less" is not a boundary. "One" is a boundary. Boundaries work better when accountability is in place. Since boundaries are susceptible to wiggle room and exceptions, we are more likely to have success when the boundary is clear and shared with someone else. Finally, boundaries are used to manage good things that have a tendency to get out of control. They are not for problem areas.

[   ]

Long ago, Jesus asked a blind man a strange question. "What do you want?" (Mark 10:36). The answer was obvious, wasn't it? Perhaps not. Blindness had its advantages. If you had been blind all your life, you probably were pretty set in certain patterns. Your food and transport probably came from consistent sources, as did your clothes. The blind man's job consisted of sitting at the roadside, waiting for someone to throw a coin or two in his cup. But that still never *healed* the man. On the other hand, if Jesus healed him, then everything would change. He would have to find a job, take care of himself, think about his future. Life would be turned upside down. But he would be able to see! So, when Jesus asked him the question, "What do you want?" the answer may not have been as obvious as it first appears. Yet, the blind man replied that he wanted to see.

The question we each have to ask ourselves is, What do I want? We can have God's feast, but not if we are too busy to come to the table. Creating space in your life will require substantial core change. Some of that change will not look particularly appealing at first. We may be exhausted, but at least we are not bored. Alcoholics Anonymous suggests that usually alcoholics will not give up alcohol until they hit bottom. Change is too scary. Sub-mediocre certainty trumps uncertainty almost every time.

Jesus offers us a path toward rest and peace and joy. This path is also full of adventure and excitement, but it may not look that way viewed from a distance. The world offers us a different path toward excitement and stimulation, promising that happiness will come along for the ride. How has that been working out for you? Who are you going to trust? The temptation will be to try to play both sides—to try renovation without demolition. Do certain things to appease God, and other things to keep a foot in the best the world has to offer. This is the classic definition of a divided person. What is too easily dismissed is that a divided person is a torn-apart person. No wonder we are overloaded and overwhelmed.

In the remaining chapters, I will paint a broad-brush canvas of what a joyful, purpose-filled, renovated life looks like. I will offer direction, without prescribing specific, turn-by-turn formulas.

I believe if we do the hard work to create space, we will finally be able to breathe again. When we learn to breathe again, we will begin to live again.

BREATHING EXERCISE

Think about the place in your life that is most overloaded. Which tool in the renovator's toolbox could help you the most in addressing your overload? Make one step in the right direction using that tool.

Key Takeaways

- Creating space so that we can breathe again is like the process of renovating a kitchen. It necessitates a plan, then demolition, and finally renovation. Renovation will not work without the hard, prior work of planning and demolition.
- The plan begins by first assessing the job. This involves an honest life assessment to discern where we are and what are the critical areas that most need our attention.
- While the work may be hard, there is joy in the journey.
- The "renovator's toolbox," the tools we will need for renovation, include these:
  - Tool #1: Dominoes. Is there one major area that needs

attention first that will create a domino effect toward relief? Is there one small area that is sabotaging the major areas in which you hope to make progress?

- Tool #2: Systems. The right systems in our lives simplify and create automatic success.
- Tool #3: Fasting. Fasting is the choice to intentionally do without something for a period of time to help break its hold and impact on our lives. Fasting can apply to food, shopping, TV, or technology.
- Tool #4: Firewall. For the more difficult sources of overload, we build a firewall into the future. This becomes a useful tool for systemic problems, such as financial overload or overcommitting.
- Tool # 5: Boundaries. Since overload comes from taking on too much, a needed tool is the use of boundaries, which serve as predetermined guardrails to keep us on course.

[5]
Redeeming Time

We must be ready to allow ourselves to be interrupted by God.

—Dietrich Bonhoeffer, *Life Together*

1,440

Here is the catch when it comes to overload and underload: it is all an illusion. We all have the exact same amount of time in each day, 1,440 minutes. You and I are not actually overloaded or underloaded. Our minutes are exactly the same. We each apportion 1,440 minutes in ways that leave us breathless and stressed, or we parcel out those same minutes in ways that invigorate and satisfy. It all comes down to the choices we make about how we spend our time and energy.

What has changed is the speed with which we plow through our 1,440 minutes. In Jesus' day, 1,440 minutes might be divided between three activities or fewer. Whole days were used in the Son of God's life walking from one town to another, a task that would take us thirty minutes today. How did He, and His disciples who followed after Him, change the world with those same 1,440 minutes when we can't even keep our own heads above water? The enigma continues. If one hundred years ago, people spent their time divided between ten different categories of activities, now we might spend our time in thirty different activities. Technology and efficiencies have allowed us to do a greater number of activities in the same amount of time. Fifty years ago, written communication traveled by what we now affectionately call "snail mail." Email brought on a communication revolution. Now, texting, which began in 1992, makes staying in touch almost instantaneous. But quantity does not equal quality, and efficiency does not equate to impact. The consequences of this real-location of time is that several of the ways we used to spend our time are now cast aside in favor of other activities. Because we now spend our minutes in a greater number of activities, we feel the torrent of breathlessly switching from one event to the next.

Overload is simply an expression of how many things we are doing and the speed with which we are executing those activities. Let me use an example.

Today, other than a few small tasks that I can knock out in about thirty minutes by car, I have only one thing to do: write this book. I will be busy for the whole day writing this book. In fact, I will probably work harder, with greater focus, on this day than on other days when I have multiple meetings, because those days invariably have lots of stops and starts and short breaks for travel and transition built in them. Of course, the multiple-meeting day feels busier. Today is more pro-ductive and efficient because I am only doing one thing, which I have decided is very important for me to do. At the end of today, I will likely be tired and satisfied. That is good. At the end of today, I will have lived 1,440 minutes, just like the busy executive or the frenetic salesperson. *Overloaded lives are the consequence of buying into the speed obsession of our culture, which elevates urgency over importance, quantity over quality, and breadth over depth.*

Here's another example. A century and a half ago, people spent on average zero hours interacting with electronic media, because it didn't exist. Today, American adults spend on average eleven hours per day interacting with some form of electronic media. How much time is good and healthy for us to spend with media? That depends on each person's specific situation. The key for me is to make sure that the time I spend with media is aligned with my true values based on the person I want to become and the kind of life I want to live. It is not to allow culture to dictate those choices. I have concluded that the choices that culture would make on my behalf would leave me breathless and bereft of what I consider worthy of my precious minutes. I have concluded that culture would have me worship at the altar of quantity and ignore areas that God says bring life.

One of the hopes of this book is that we will choose to examine what we are giving our lives to. As part of that reflection, I hope we will also become aware of what we are sacrificing to these new demands on our time. Past generations did not have to struggle with these choices. They did not exist. In another five or ten years, new opportunities will arise, asserting their claim on our 1,440 minutes. Each day we choose how we will spend our 1,440 minutes.

What we need is a new paradigm regarding time. How might we see time differently such that we lean more easily into life-giving uses of our days?

BREATHING EXERCISE

Make a quick list of the different activities that consumed your minutes this past week. On a scale of 1 to 10, how do those activities align with your values? Reflect on your activities and rating.

A New Take on Time

Our lives are made up of weeks, days, hours, minutes, and seconds. We use that time well or poorly. Hundreds of books have been written to teach us how to manage our time better. I feel as if I've read them all. Usually, managing time means fitting more activity into less time. In this sense, learning to manage time becomes part of the problem of overload, because we convince ourselves that the core problem is our inability to do two hours of work in one hour. Perhaps more than any other area over these thirty years of addressing overload, time has been my focus. I have concluded that we don't need to manage time better; we need a completely new paradigm for time. We need to redeem the time we have.

In the New Testament, two different Greek words are used to describe time. *Chronos* is used to describe minutes, hours, and days. *Kairos* is used to describe the concept of appropriate season, opportunity, and the proper time. It is the word used when Jesus said, "The time is fulfilled, and the kingdom of God is at hand" (Mark 1:15 NKJV). In the early chapters of John, Jesus said, "My time is not yet fulfilled." (John 7:8 GNV). Kairos is more than clock time; it is the right time. Minutes and hours matter, but quality of life is experienced in kairos time. Think about that special dinner you had recently with good friends or your children. We measure and manage chronos; we experience kairos. When we spend kairos time, we get the sense that minutes and hours are standing still. Kairos time makes an indelible impression on our memory. I think of special breakfasts that I have shared with best friends, and date nights with Weezie. I remember rounds of golf with Chris and Alex, and sitting on the porch, crying with a close friend who lost his brother. I think of times lost in the splendor of worship. This is life at its richest that makes managing minutes seem shallow. But in our culture chronos crowds out kairos. We allow our schedules and tasks lists to become so full that kairos time, which is never urgent, gets eliminated.

As we move through this next part of our life renovation, we will move in the counterintuitive direction of deemphasizing our chronos and elevating kairos, where life is found. The goal will be to fill our lives with so many life-giving experiences that we don't have time to waste or squander in lesser activities or distractions.

In preparation for our work, I want to encourage you to think of the last time you experienced kairos time. Was it on a vacation? Was it a lingering meal? Perhaps you were lost in a great book. Relive it! Isn't that what you desire most? If it is difficult for you to think of a kairos moment or that time was too long ago, be encouraged that the work of renovation will create the space for time to be redeemed, for chronos to be filled with more kairos.

BREATHING EXERCISE

Take your activity list from the last exercise and put a *C* by each one that was a "chronos" activity, and a *K* by each activity you would call a "kairos" activity. Did kairos fit into your week?

Framing the Day

So, where do we begin in our effort to redeem time? How do we move from defense, living frantically by the clock, to offense, where healing occurs?

We begin at the beginning, the first hours of the day. How we begin the day sets the stage for how we continue the day. And yet, for so many, the beginning of the day starts off at a sprint. We all have a routine, however short or exacting, with which we begin and end each day. Think of it as a frame. Frames add so much to a picture.

The right frame makes a painting pop, bringing out the most vivid colors. Without a frame, many pictures seem naked and bland. In reality, the better the painting, the more important the frame.

Why is it, then, that we give so little thought, time, and intention to how we begin our days? The quality of our first hour dramatically impacts the quality of our whole day.

The beginning of our day is a blank slate. Except in that challenging stage with infants and small children, we choose what time we wake up and how we wake up. Even in that difficult season of child-rearing, we often have some control over how we shape that first imperfect hour. We choose what we do in the first moments and when and how we transition from the beginning to the substance of the day.

I had the morning routine down to a science in my twenties. I knew exactly the time my foot needed to exit the front door, and what was the minimum amount of time it would take me to cross that threshold—twenty minutes. As soon as the alarm went off, I popped out of the bed and sprinted to the shower. After showering, brushing my teeth, dressing, and eating a bowl of cereal, I was crossing the finish line at the front door like someone who just finished the Boston Marathon. It didn't matter what time I needed to get started at work, whether it was seven thirty or eight or nine o'clock. I would simply count backwards twenty minutes from when I needed to leave the house, and that was when I set my alarm. I justified this because I was always tired and needed every minute of sleep I could squeeze out of the night before. Needless to say, this did not help my day or my productivity get off on the right foot.

I finally tired of always racing and always being exhausted. So, I introduced a frame to the day. The frame was a thin one to begin with, an extra ten minutes to get my bearings, read a very quick chapter of Scripture or a devotional, say a token prayer, and then race on. It felt like a huge sacrifice, but I knew it was better than what I had done before. At first, I felt so exhausted, as if I had crawled out of bed two hours earlier. I persisted, and even began to widen my morning frame an extra thirty minutes. While this was not a major game changer, I could tell it was a step in the right direction.

The time came when I finally realized that the frame has a top and a bottom, a beginning of the day and an end of the day. I was exhausted at the beginning of the day because of how I'd ended the day before. If anyone had asked me in those days, I would have confidently asserted that I was a night owl. My best time of the day was night. It wasn't true though. I only stayed up late because I had conditioned myself to stay up late. Nothing of quality happened late. I was not creative, productive, or particularly relational. Mostly, I watched TV. That part of the frame needed changing.

Dissatisfaction and a lot of reading about margin caused me to build a slightly wider frame for my days. The wider frame helped make the painting of the day a little more beautiful. At night, I went to sleep a little earlier and watched a little less TV. In the mornings, I spent a little more time with God before I walked out the door.

The frame has become precious to me. Now I love my early mornings and enjoy more peaceful nights. My internal engine idles more slowly. Not surprisingly, my productivity has increased. My days are more thought-out. My goals are clearer, my activity more focused. Obviously, regular snags occur—unavoidable late nights that bleed into shorter mornings, stressful periods that erode the calm of the days or evenings. But regardless of the good times and the harder times, I am always confident that I am better with a well-framed day than with the alternative frenetic day devoid of a frame.

Getting Practical

Ideas are great, but unless we are practical, the ideas will remain only theory. How do we make real change and real progress in this critical area?

Begin your morning the night before. In my case, all of my best intentions regarding getting up earlier and having a meaningful morning routine were sabotaged the night before. Thinking myself a night owl, I let my nights drag out until late, usually with pretty worthless activities: a late football game, surfing the internet (always a bad idea late at night, when defenses are low), reading a novel, or playing some online game (like *Words with Friends*). Mindless activities lured me late into the night. Once my nights were extended until 11:00 or midnight or later, the possibility of a meaningful morning was shot.

The mornings begin the night before! Most of us need a minimum of seven or eight hours of sleep to function well the next day. That means if I go to sleep at 11:00 p.m., the earliest I can wake up the next morning and hope to perform well is 6:00 a.m., which assumes I fall asleep as soon as the lights go out. If I go to sleep at midnight, then 7:00 a.m. Certainly, the quality of our sleep is a factor too, but a certain quantity of sleep is the beginning point before we can worry about quality. I should mention that when we change our internal clocks, it may take a few weeks for that change to take root. During those few weeks, we are likely to be tired in the morning. We need to push through for a short while until we adjust. We are more adaptable as human beings than we believe or like to admit.

Make your morning time primarily me-and-God time. If we only use the extra time we create in the morning for work and productivity, then it won't be long before we will opt for a little extra sleep. Mornings are my special time between me and God. Our precious morning time should become our favorite, most enjoyable time of the day. Once it becomes that, and not an obligation or strict discipline, then we've won the battle. I now treasure my unrushed time to think, journal, pray, read, and yes, prepare for the day ahead.

Nothing will change our lives more fundamentally than growing deeper in love with Christ. Intimacy with Christ may seem unrelated to the rest of our productive lives, but the connection is much more direct than we realize. Give Him the time He deserves.

Take small bites, and then increase your appetite. For most people, massive, radical changes made all at once are not sustainable. If you are just beginning to make time for yourself in the morning, start with a manageable amount of time. For some, this may be fifteen minutes; for others, this may mean thirty minutes. It needs to be enough to actually make a difference, but not so much that it won't stick as a habit.

Be flexible and creative with your morning time. Once you conquer the hurdle of creating morning space for you and God, be wildly creative and flexible with how you use that precious gift. That time is to enjoy and savor. One person may take a prayer walk. Another may journal in great depth. One may go deep in the Scriptures or read the spiritual classics. One answer does not fit all. Some people experience, hear, and learn from God best through nature. Others connect with God through worship, Scripture, or silence. We should use our morning times to walk with God in whatever manner we deem best. This will likely change in different seasons of our lives. When we give ourselves the freedom to enjoy our morning time, then we will be establishing this time for the long haul.

Extend your frame for the day to your evening. Improve both ends of the frame, the mornings and the evenings. Evenings can be incredibly rich and relaxing times. What a shame that so many people simply turn them into an extension of their productive workdays. Life is more than work. Down the line, I doubt any of us will regret not working more evenings! Evenings are great for relationships, whether with family or friends. They are a perfect time to wind down with a book or with a good TV show. There are so many creative ways to use evenings well. As you think about your evenings, ask yourself, "Is the way I am using my evening restorative and life-giving?" If not, begin the process of making small tweaks to move in that direction.

Two Final Caveats

Some people are actual night owls. I talked with one such person recently who does her very best creative work late at night. If you are convinced that you are truly a night owl, then frame your day accordingly. Give generous margin at night, when you are at your best. Mornings are still important. They are still part of the frame, though how you spend that morning time may look different from most people. The principle of framing the day still holds true. For the night owl, a well-executed morning of planning and preparation will make the quality of the evenings so much better.

Secondly, certain seasons of life make framing the day well extremely difficult. Seasons of unusual demand at work, crying babies, and young children challenge our ability to create any frame. If you are in one of those seasons, give yourself plenty of grace. Don't abandon the frame, but realize that seasons change. Enjoy the season you are in. Bring God into the misshapen frame of your day.

BREATHING EXERCISE

Write down your current morning and evening routine. What is one specific way to improve the quality of each of these routines?

Slow Down

Many years ago, I played in a charity golf tournament raising money for a Christian organization, Young Life. These events typically have gimmick holes to spice up the competition. In this particular tournament, on one of the short holes, they had a race. The goal was not to have the lowest score but to complete the hole in the shortest time—without using a cart! The hole measured about 180 yards around a pond. The contest was to hit the ball, sprint around the pond, and continue hitting the ball as fast as possible until it was in the hole, at which point the clock would stop. The trick was balancing fast play with quality shots. As I mentioned earlier, I tend to be very competitive, so this contest was right up my alley. I was younger then and still had a sprint or two in me. I saw the times that came in before me and thought I had a good chance. The clock started. I hit a good shot onto the green and took off. By the time I flew around the lake, I was completely out of breath. I grabbed my putter, made a quick swat at the ball, knocked the putt to about two feet, and holed out with a tremendous time. I thought my time could not be beat—until my brother stepped up behind me. He is a few years older than I, so I wasn't worried about him running much faster. He hit his first shot well (he is a very good golfer) and ran quickly around the lake to hit his putt. He stepped up to the putt and drained it for a score of two and beat my time.

Now, we are not in terrible shape. But what I also remember about that contest was that for the next few holes, after sprinting around that lake, we were ruined. Our golf was terrible until we could recover from the speed contest.

Golf is not meant for speed; neither is life! Speed kills! Consider the impact of speed. A NASCAR driver races around the track at top speeds. The speed is exhilarating and exciting . . . and dangerous. Cars racing at those speeds wear down quickly. Tires have to be changed every few laps. The fans see the excitement of fast cars, but speed comes at a cost. Cars break down, needing to be rebuilt constantly because of the wear of driving at such high speed.

The same holds true for us. When we move fast, we make more mistakes, wear out more quickly, and risk the health consequences that accompany stressed-out living.

In contrast, when I slow down, I enjoy life so much more. Almost inevitably, a better pace creates better focus and a more relaxed atmosphere. Ironically, slowing down does not result in getting less done.

Slowing Down and Moving Fast

When considering the speed at which you live life, there are two important considerations. Knowing these things will help you decide whether you want to move fast, or slooooow doooown: There is a time for moving fast and a time for slowing down. Some menial tasks are worth flying through. The problem comes when speed becomes our default way of living. As we begin to learn the benefits of slowing our speed, we build our discernment muscles that enable us to decide when it is best to move quickly and when we should let ourselves ease the pace.

Slowing down is a revolutionary way to improve productivity while enjoying the process. Speed is overrated. We have been duped into thinking that we need to move fast, when in reality, we would be better off if we moved more slowly, with relaxed focus. Consider this: If I am driving ten miles in a straight line to an appointment at fifty miles per hour, I will arrive at my destination in twelve minutes. If I drive at forty miles per hour, I will arrive in fifteen minutes. That's three minutes' savings. If there are stoplights along the way, the time savings will be less since I cannot maintain the ten-mile-per-hour differential the whole way. In other words, rushing to an appointment ten miles away may save me an amazing one to three minutes of time. Hardly worth the rush.

There are additional reasons to slow down:

- **Slowing down creates clarity.** When I am operating in hyper-speed, I waste time trying to figure out what I have to do next without actually doing the next thing. When I slow down, I gain clarity about what is essential, what can be postponed, and what doesn't even need doing.
- **Slowing down increases focus.** When I am rushing, the quality of my work declines substantially. Inevitably, I end up redoing tasks several times. Those times I enter my duties with a calm spirit, the quality of the work improves, and because I have a calm focus, it takes less time.
- **Slowing down improves quality.** I can't count the number of times I have had to redo work because I rushed through the process and made unnecessary mistakes. I am famous for trying to take shortcuts, like putting furniture together without consulting the instructions. Every time, I get one piece wrong, forcing me to start all over again. When I am unrushed, I make fewer mistakes, which saves me time.
- **Slowing down is enjoyable.** I love slowing down! I love the feeling of not rushing and enjoying the present moment. It makes me feel like everything is going to be okay. Slowing down, once we get used to it, puts life into proper perspective.

Moving fast is a bad habit. We look at the speedometer in our cars and realize, without even thinking about it, that we are going fifteen miles per hour over the speed limit. We race through our days and realize we are tense, jittery, and can't even remember what we did an hour ago. On the one hand, moving fast makes us feel important. Why else would we be so busy unless we were critical to the survival of the world? On the other hand, we hate the feeling of always being out of breath. We are tired people.

How do we slow down? We slow down by changing a few small, bad habits at a time. We slow down by becoming aware that we are going so terribly fast. We slow down by confessing that we are tired of the pace we are living and want to live differently. Here are a few practical thoughts:

- **Begin by slowing down your morning.** Even if you have to get up thirty minutes earlier, begin the day moving slowly. Take time to breathe, to pray, to plan, to say "good morning" to those around you.

- **Plan your day with a little more space in between appointments and meetings.** You may be surprised how those few extra minutes help you catch your breath, be more prepared, improve your mood, and even improve your overall productivity.

- **Don't pull out your phone at every free moment.** When we fill our free moments with our phones, we, in essence, lose our free moments. This leaves us with a sense that we are always busy, which creates stress.

- **Learn to linger.** This is the secret sauce of slow. For me, it means giving plenty of margin for scheduled activities, including my quiet time. Margin creates the inevitable opportunity to linger. *Our problem in life isn't that we don't have enough time in each day; it is that we don't have enough quality in each day.* Learning to linger with God in the morning and then with people throughout the day increases the odds that more of our days will be filled with meaningful experiences. This is kairos living as opposed to chronos living. Joy is found in lingering. Think about it. When have you ever experienced joy while rushing? Aren't your richest, most joyful memories ones that occurred while lingering? I think of long, unrushed dinners with close friends and leisurely rounds of golf when nothing was scheduled after the round. I think of relaxed days on the beach. I remember long ago canoeing on a lake for hours. The common denominator in all of these experiences is unrushed time, when nothing scheduled after the event forced me to watch the clock and diluted the pleasure. I know that this is a luxury we can't experience every day, but we can understand what the ingredients of joy are and move in that direction more often. Why not? The reality is, many of us will not allow ourselves this luxury because we feel too guilty relaxing when there is so much to be done. We are content to be constantly discontent, rather than testing the waters of a better way. Life will go on if we take an afternoon off or if we linger at the dinner table for an extra thirty minutes. No one will condemn us if we enjoy ourselves for a few moments. No need to post the experience on social media. Just enjoy life in an unrushed, happy way. When we give ourselves the permission to experience joy, we alter our perspective of what matters. Certainly, being productive in our work and what we are called to do is important, but there is more to life than productivity.

If you are tired of being tired, try slowing down. Make one change and see how it feels. If it feels good, then add another. With a little time, you may find yourself getting more done and enjoying the scenery along the way.

BREATHING EXERCISE

For one day, arrive early everywhere you go, and drive slowly getting to those places. Journal about whether the experience was enjoyable or annoying.

Slow Living

Once we learn to slow down the overall pace at which we live, we take the next step. Embrace slow living. Slow living is time's version of minimalism. Slow living is kairos living. Here's where we learn that we need more than slowing down. If we truly want to experience abundant living, we need to do different things.

Slow living is a companion concept to slowing down. I define slow living as "prioritizing activities that specifically benefit from an unrushed pace." I believe that the quality of our days is directly correlated with the inclusion of slow-living activities. Following is a small sampling of what I would call slow activities:

- **Reading books.** Reading, in general, tends to be a slow activity, but in our day of online overload, quick skimming has become the norm. The process of reading a book slows this down. Books are designed as a deep dive, whether it is a novel, a biography, or a self-help book. The deep dive combined with the slowness of reading page after page is an additional benefit. Let's take that concept one step further. When I read a great book, I also highlight the book. I read most of my nonfiction books on a Kindle because I can highlight the book, download the highlighted sections, and keep them for later, easy reference. With my favorite books, I go even further. I take my highlights and structure them into an outline in Word. By doing this, I go from reading a book to internalizing the book. I don't do this often, but when I do, that book takes deep root in me. That may seem slow and tedious, but if my goal is to change, the extra time is totally worth it.

- **Dining.** Notice that I didn't say eating. A slow meal with people you care about, void of technological distraction, feeds the soul as well as the body. One thing about slow dining, it needs to be coupled with the right place. Most restaurants are wired to move people along quickly, "turning over the tables" so that they can maximize the revenue. A few places embrace people who want to take their time. The atmosphere of these special places reflects the higher goal of creating a memorable experience. Even slow meals alone, perhaps with a good book, work wonders in combating the angst and rush of the typical day. Is it worth it to rush through our food just so that we can rush to the next place? How much happier would we be if we added a few relaxed dining experiences, whether at home or in a restaurant, into our weekly routine?

- **Rest and relaxation.** Real rest has been replaced by distraction, stimulation, and obsession with more. Unfortunately, rest is a lost art. We vegetate in front of the TV or lose ourselves in a video game, both of which are fine in moderation. The problem comes when these are our only forms of relaxation. Good sleep, relaxing leisure, and even an occasional nap is a wonderful luxury that everyone should prize. Here's a confession from a driven person: I have a very hard time relaxing. It doesn't come naturally to me. This is where slow living is so helpful to me. As we build the other slow activities into our lives, we will find the ability to relax returning. Eventually, I don't have to think about relaxing, I am relaxing because the things I am choosing to do are relaxing. I need to retrain myself, because everything around me is working to train me to go fast, be distracted, and resign myself to anxious living.

- **Play.** A cousin to the value of rest is the importance of play. Stuart Brown, in the book *Play: How It Shapes the Brain, Opens the Imagination, and Invigorates the Soul,* argues that play is so much more than a luxury. He asserts, "I have found that remembering what play is and making it part of our daily lives are probably the most important factors in being a fulfilled human being."[1] We must challenge culture's wisdom that suggests that one-track, driven focus is the optimal path to purpose and happiness.

Balance is needed when thinking about slow living. A life filled only with slow-living activities threatens to settle us in a comfort zone that misses out on the adventure God has for us. The benefits from these slow-living activities are enjoyed most when interspersed with vibrant productivity. The rhythm between slow and active, reflective and industrious, makes life more interesting and even more fruitful. Running hard all day without a break and without variety may spike our stimulation meters, but that kind of life is neither sustainable nor pleasurable.

BREATHING EXERCISE

Name two slow-living activities and schedule them into the week ahead of you.

The Work-Life Dance

Redeeming time is always a balancing act. We wish we could take our time and linger and spend endless hours with those we love, but we have responsibilities that demand our attention.

The internet is littered with articles on mastering work-life balance. I've thought long and hard about this concept. Yes, we need balance. Balancing the demands of a career and all the other demands that flood our way is complex. Beyond the complexity, though, is a deception implied by the whole concept of work-life balance.

The very concept of work-life balance implies pitting work against life. Isn't work a part of life? Shouldn't work be life-giving, instead of the negative side of the seesaw of life? The problem shows itself in two different forms. First, work has too large a place in many of our lives, either because we love our work and spend too much time in it, our identity is too tied into what we do, or work's demands are so substantial that we cannot wrangle it. Second, even if our time commitment to work is not out of balance, our energy commitment is. We come home exhausted because work demands the best of our energy. I have never heard the debate center around life edging out our need to work. Work is always the problem! It is always what needs balancing!

Why is it that I have such a hard time getting control of the demands of my work? Is it my boss? Is it how work feeds my ego and my need for stimulation? Is my identity too wrapped up in what I do? Am I avoiding other, more difficult issues outside of work?

What does the struggle communicate about my priorities? Am I neglecting my family to provide for my family? Have I elevated money and status to an inappropriate place in my life that is requiring me to agree to demands that violate my values? Difficult questions.

As we work to wrangle our work demands, we might ask, Are there creative ways to be more efficient without sacrificing effectiveness at our jobs? Can we negotiate, either with ourselves or with our bosses, to make more room for that which we would clearly say is more important in our life?

I know that these are hard issues.

Perhaps a helpful way to reframe the problem is to rename it from "work-life balance," implying a constant balancing act, to "work-life dance." Those I know who seem to be winning the struggle treat it as a dance. They know that sometimes work will be demanding. Sometimes home or church will be demanding. They dance, not tiptoe, through times and seasons, but never take their eye off the bigger picture of who they are and what matters the most to them.

Remember, just because the struggle is real doesn't mean we should give in and admit defeat. Even a small change can have a huge impact. A little progress, which can come from a slight shift in perspective, may be a tipping point creating a better flow between work and the rest of life. Getting a handle on the demands of work may be the major domino that topples the other dominoes that are choking out life.

I encourage you to adopt the following resolutions:

- *Resolved: I will not allow my life to continue to be dictated by the urgent, crowding out the important.*

- *Resolved: I will clarify the priorities of my life and live accordingly.*

- *Resolved: I will not give my friends and my family the leftovers of my energy and attention.*

- *Resolved: I will accept that just because periods of time get out of balance does not mean life is out of balance. Balance shows itself over long spans of time.*

- *Resolved: I will accept that the tension between work and the rest of life is an imperfect dance, not a predictable formula.*

- *Resolved: I will reframe work as a vital part of life, not a necessary evil.*

- *Resolved: I will no longer put off creating the life I want to live because it is too difficult.*

Our lives are meant to be a beautiful tapestry, with work, family, mission, health, and growth creating one whole magnificent masterpiece.

BREATHING EXERCISE

Write a paragraph about how you are managing the work-life dance. Include why you dance as you do and how you want to dance differently going forward.

Establishing Rhythm

Once we have done the hard work of reducing rush, we now focus on establishing life-giving rhythm. Think of great music. Rhythm is essential. The music speeds up and slows down. It has crescendos that lift us up and then gradually softens to draw us in. Our days and weeks need this sort of pleasing rhythm.

Incorporating rhythm doesn't mean going slowly all the time, nor does it mean always staying the same speed. Rhythm means creating a pleasing pacing throughout the day. When I am successful at this, I am both more content and more effective.

What are ways to find your rhythm? At the risk of being repetitive, *rhythm begins by starting your day right.* The beginning of the day dictates the tenor of the whole day. Think of your favorite song. The beginning of a song is critical. Every song has an intentional beginning that flows into what is to come. Here are some other suggestions:

Know your Best Time for Your Best Results

Every person has his or her most effective times of the day and his or her less productive moments. Know when you are at your best, and plan your days accordingly. Personally, I have learned that mornings are best for my writing, and afternoons are best for my meetings. Contrary to most expert advice, I schedule my exercise at the end of the day. That creates the best rhythm for me.

Consider Your Weekly Rhythm

A week is a good unit of time in which to make meaningful progress. A week is like your favorite playlist. The playlist has a purpose,
whether it is variety, mood, or theme. When I clarify what my priorities are a week at a time, and review those priorities daily, my
days go smoother. I worry less about a day filled with busy work
when I know the next day will be when I leap ahead in the areas
that matter.

When Possible, Vary Your Speed Throughout the Day

When I have a full day of back-to-back meetings, I end the day
exhausted. Sometimes that can't be helped. But if I plan my week
well, I can usually vary the pace of each day with some thoughtful
and some relational times, some intense and some more relaxing
activities. This allows me to be very productive over a full week
without totally exhausting myself.

Balance Fast with Slow

The busier I am, the slower I go. Whenever I find myself tensing up
and speeding up, I take a deep breath and consciously slow down.
To this day, I have never felt as though this reduced my effectiveness. On the contrary, slowing down helps me work at my best.

End Your Day Well

Pay attention to your evenings, particularly the last hour or so
before bedtime. An enjoyable evening counters a hectic day. Also,
a good evening sets the stage for the next morning to begin well.

Some people like rock music; some like jazz. Music and rhythm
are a personal preference. The key is to find the music and rhythm
that sync with the way God made you.

Rhythm doesn't happen by accident. Great rhythm is the result of intentional effort. Its reward is spacious beginnings and gentle endings that allow for great middles.

BREATHING EXERCISE

Rhythm is intentional. What one step can you make to improve the rhythm of your day or week?

The Sabbath Principle

I love Eugene Peterson's translation of Matthew 11:28–30 in *The Message.*

> Are you tired? Worn out? Burned out on religion? Come to me. Get away with me and you'll recover your life. I'll show you how to take a real rest. Walk with me and work with me—watch how I do it. Learn the unforced rhythms of grace. I won't lay anything heavy or ill-fitting on you. Keep company with me and you'll learn to live freely and lightly.

Seems too good to be true. Why does this sweet call, this tender offering, seem so impossible to us? Have we relegated our faith as a means to become better, more productive, successful people, and nothing more? Perhaps part of the problem goes all the way back to the beginning, to something very simple that we have lost.

Seven days of creation. That is not a lot of time to do everything that needs to be done. One would think that with only seven days, each day would be chock-full of activity and priorities, with hardly a moment to breathe. Yet this is not what we see. We see in the seven days this "good" crescendo building through the first six days to the "very good," cymbals-crashing creation of man and woman. And then there was the seventh day, and nothing happened. God rested. Who would ever think that a full day of rest would make the list for the seven days of creation?

Fast-forward to God and Moses and the Ten Commandments. Only ten! Surely these ten must be the penultimate of do's and don'ts. The list is surprising though. It begins with "You shall have no other gods before me" (Deut. 5:7). Makes sense as a top-ten commandment. No idols and not taking the Lord's name in vain are the next two. Then a big surprise. "Observe the Sabbath day by keeping it holy" (v. 12). It goes on from there with an extremely detailed description of what keeping the Sabbath holy looks like. It is by far the longest and most detailed of all the Ten Commandments. It is as if God knew that we would have a hard time with this one and would find all sorts of ways to skirt the commandment. The rest of the commandments proceed from there.

Why is it that this commandment ranks as the least considered of all the commandments? This should be the most delightful, easiest of all the commandments to keep, and yet we struggle so much with it that it has also become the most ignored commandment.

Fast-forward once again to the days of the prophet Isaiah. The nation of Israel continued to vacillate back and forth in their faithfulness to God. In the midst of this, Isaiah addressed core issues and core promises with Israel in his prophetic voice.

> "If you keep your feet from breaking the Sabbath and from doing as you please on my holy day, if you call the Sabbath a delight and the Lord's holy day honorable, and if you honor it by not going your own way and not doing as you please or speaking idle words, then you will find joy in the Lord, and I will cause you to ride in triumph on the heights of the land and to feast on the inheritance of your father Jacob." For the mouth of the LORD has spoken. (Is. 58:13–14)

There's something crazy about this promise from the mouth of God. In essence, God was saying, "If you will rest from your labors one day per week and honor Me, then I will give you unspeakable joy, the heights of the land, and the best of my feasts." Isn't joy one of those "best of life" things that we are constantly trying to figure out? Here, God tells us specifically how to find it. Honor and keep the Sabbath. Will we believe God? Will we even try to obey one of the plainest of His Ten Commandments?

When Weezie and I came to our epiphany about the toxic nature of overload that we had allowed into our lives almost thirty years ago, one of the very first steps we implemented was observing the Sabbath. It didn't feel practical at the time; we were already overloaded. If seven days were not enough to get everything done, how would we get by with only six days? But we were desperate. The first few weeks were comical. Weezie and I would take turns watching the kids, while the other one napped. We had no energy to rest. All we could do was catch up on sleep. Still, that simple permission to sleep gave us a glimmer of hope that things could be different. Eventually, we moved beyond sleeping the Sabbath away to enjoying the Sabbath.

Within a short period, the Sabbath became our refuge. Instead of TGIF, we embraced TGISunday. Since then, we have imperfectly practiced the Sabbath for almost three decades. As I reflect now, I don't know that I ever would have learned to breathe again without Sabbath playing a central role.

What Does "Keeping the Sabbath" Mean?

Volumes have been written on this. Judaism has debated the finer points for thousands of years. I am no expert. I still struggle with the best way to rest, but I think there are some basics that represent a good start.

First, keeping the Sabbath means not working. What is work? Work is in the eye of the beholder. For me, gardening is definitely work. For Weezie, gardening is restful and joyful. Certain kinds of reading for me are work, and certain kinds are restful. Going to the driving range is restful for me. For many it would be agony. Clearly, emailing, preparing for the week, and grinding away at my computer are all versions of work. We have to check our spirits and examine our hearts to determine what is work for us—and what is restful.

Second, Sabbath is a time to rest. Rest means more than catching up on sleep, although that is not a bad place to start. Rest means de-stressing. On the Sabbath, we purposely cast away the things that bring us stress. While that is easier said than done, we can intentionally leave those issues that cause us stress for another day. We may be very imperfect in this area, but any progress toward less stress is good progress.

Third, Sabbath is a day for joy. Too many of us have forgotten what joy feels like. Part of that is because we never stop grinding. When we center on joy, we center on people and on God. With no work to do, we finally have time to have fun. We play games. We swim. We read a novel. We watch a movie. For twenty-four hours, we get off the frenetic freeway and take a deep breath and smile.

Once we are a few weeks or months into practicing the Sabbath, we will wonder how we ever survived without it.

[   ]

Because this area is so difficult for us to implement, I am going to get highly practical. Making this a part of your weekly routine takes great thought and intentionality.

Watch out for these Sabbath killers:

- Trying to practice the "spirit" of Sabbath without specific associated actions. I need specific guardrails, like no email. Otherwise, I slip, until there is no difference from other days.
- Not getting broad buy-in. Husbands and wives need to be on the same page, giving each other Sabbath rest. Involve the kids and friends in your Sabbath ways.
- Becoming legalistic. While Jesus said, "The Sabbath was made for man" (Mark 2:27), He also severely criticized the Pharisees, who hypocritically made the Sabbath all about rules, with no heart.

Decide when is the best time for you to take a sabbath rest. Though the Jewish tradition practices the Sabbath from Friday at sundown to Saturday sundown, we chose to observe the day as our schedule allowed. For those in ministry, it is probably not Sunday. I like to practice sabbath rest from sundown Saturday until sundown Sunday. This allows Weezie and me to have a built-in date night Saturday night, enjoy worship on Sunday morning, and then relax Sunday afternoon. Then, if necessary, I can glance at my schedule and workweek ahead on Sunday night for a few minutes. I love the rhythm of this sabbath practice.

The encouragement here is to move in the right direction. If this seems impractical to you because of your lifestyle and commitments, then what does seem practical? Can you practice a sabbath hour or a sabbath afternoon? Can you lean toward sabbath by moving away from technology for a few hours?

My strong encouragement to you with regard to Sabbath is to make a first step. Lean in to Sabbath. Don't worry about getting it perfect. Perfect is the territory of Pharisees. Sabbath is God's generous gift to you and me. It is time to open that gift.

BREATHING EXERCISE

If you have never practiced the Sabbath, decide on a baby step to try this week—maybe two hours when you stop working. If you observe the Sabbath, think about how you might improve your practice by including more joy and more rest in the day.

Key Takeaways

- Overload and underload are both illusions. Everyone has the same 1,440 minutes each day. Our experience of overload is a feeling resulting from the choices of how we use our 1,440 minutes.
- Chronos time is minutes, hours, and days. Kairos time is experiences and the "right" time. Our goal is to live more in the awareness of kairos, and less by the tyranny of the clock.
- The frame that we put at the beginning of the day and the end of the day affects the beauty in the middle of the day. Intentionally creating a meaningful frame helps gain a sense of control over the chaos within each day. Tips:
  - Begin your morning the night before.
  - Make your morning time primarily me-and-God time.
  - Take small bites, and then increase your appetite.
  - Be flexible and creative with your morning time.
  - Extend your frame for the day to your evening.
- Slowing down is a counterintuitive way of becoming more productive.
  - Slowing down creates clarity.
  - Slowing down increases focus.
  - Slowing down improves quality.
  - Slowing down is enjoyable.
  - Tips:
    - Begin by slowing down your morning.
    - Plan your day with a little more space between appointments and meetings.
    - Don't pull out your phone at every free moment.
    - Learn to linger.
- Slow living is prioritizing activities that specifically benefit from an unrushed pace.
  - Slow-living activities
    - Reading books

- Dining
- Rest and relaxation
- Play
- Work-life balance is better thought of as a dance, where we move smoothly around all of life's demands, always keeping our attention on what deeply matters.
- Rhythm is critical in our efforts to overcome overload. Rhythm implies different paces at different times.
  - Rhythm begins by starting your day right.
  - Know the best time for your best results.
  - Consider your weekly rhythm.
  - When possible, vary your speed throughout the day.
  - Balance fast with slow.
  - End your day well.
- The Sabbath is a life-giving, neglected command of God given for our benefit. It means choosing for twenty-four hours not to work, however we might define work. It infuses rest in a tidal wave of busyness.

[6]

Creating Space

In the spiritual life, the word *discipline* means "the effort to create
some space in which God can act." Discipline means to prevent
everything in your life from being filled up. Discipline means that
somewhere you're not occupied, and certainly not preoccupied.
In the spiritual life, discipline means to create that space in which
something can happen that you hadn't planned on or counted on.

—Henri Nouwen[1]

Our Places Without Spaces

When I was in seminary many years ago, one of the areas of
study required was Greek. I learned early on that in the original Greek manuscripts of the New Testament, all the letters
were capitalized, with no spaces between the words. Before the
translators could even begin translating, they had to discern where
the breaks were between words. The original manuscripts also had
no punctuation or paragraphs. So, the translators had a substantial
task to undertake before they even started to decipher the meaning
of the text. Most of the time the process of figuring out the breaks
between words and the appropriate punctuation was obvious, but
it took quite a bit of effort before the translators could even begin
understanding what the passage was trying to say.

Consider for a moment the paragraph you just read without punctuation and spaces. It would look like this:

WHENIWASINSEMINARYMANYYEARSAGOONE
OFTHEAREASOFSTUDYWASGREEKILEARNED
EARLYONTHATINTHEORIGINALGREEKMANU-
SCRIPTSOFTHENEWTESTAMENTALLTHELETTERS
WERECAPITALIZEDWITHNOSPACESBETWEEN
THEWORDSBEFORETHETRANSLATORSCOULD
EVENBEGINTRANSLATINGTHEYHADTODISCERN
WHERETHEBREAKSWEREBETWEENWORDSTHE
ORIGINALMANUSCRIPTSALSOHADNOPUNCTUA-
TIONORPARAGRAPHSSOTHETRANSLATORSHAD
ASUBSTANTIALTASKTOUNDERTAKEBEFORETHEY
EVENSTARTEDTODECIPHERTHEMEANINGOFTHE
TEXTMOSTOFTHETIMETHEPROCESSOFFIGURING
OUTTHEBREAKSBETWEENWORDSANDTHE
APPROPRIATEPUNCTUATIONWASOBVIOUSBUTIT
TOOKQUITEABITOFEFFORTBEFORETHETRANSLA-
TORSCOULDEVENBEGINUNDERSTANDINGWHAT
THEPASSAGEWASTRYINGTOSAY

While this paragraph took up slightly less space, it was much harder to understand, if you even took the time to try to understand it. Space gives context. Space makes the undecipherable comprehensible. No matter how much we try to deny it, space makes life more livable.

Creating space in our lives is more complex than we might first imagine. For instance, we may lack space in our schedules because our job demands so much time. Yet, we can't afford to change jobs because our mortgage is so large. Where is the problem? Is it the schedule, the job, or the mortgage, or all three? Another example: We may feel constantly exhausted from the moment our eyes open until our heads hit the pillow. Is this emotional exhaustion from a draining relationship, a particular personal crisis, or is it a function of too much to do and too much clutter in our brains?

Why do some people actually have plenty of space in their lives, and yet they feel that persistent angst and restlessness as if they were completely overwhelmed?

Simple answers will not suffice. The issues are broad, touching every area of our lives. They are numerous, causing us to be confused about where to begin. They tempt us to give up before we start. Deep soul-searching is required to uncover the root problem and not only address symptoms.

Creating space is an extremely difficult task. Hard decisions are required. Habits must be broken. Internal honesty is a necessity. It takes much more time than we might expect to make these core changes and reap the benefits. Even then, culture lures us back into the fray with some new gadget that is supposed to save us time, but in reality, consumes the little free time we have. Add to this that each new stage of life comes with its own unique challenges, forcing us to solve the problem all over again. As we delve deeper, layers to the issues appear that we may not have even considered.

BREATHING EXERCISE

Compare a few books you enjoy and note how the spacing contributes to or inhibits your enjoyment. How is your life spaced?

Clutter, Clutter, Everywhere

Since our kitchen renovation is finished now, we are starting on the decluttering of the basement. Well, that is not exactly true. In reality, our kitchen has been finished for a while, but we haven't been able to muster the courage to tackle the basement. Every time we go into that nightmare of a space, we get this sick feeling of defeat. The task seems too enormous. Piles and piles of saved items that we might want one day, the kids might want, or the kids or the eventual grandkids might enjoy, fill our basement storage to the rafters. I think there might even be piles for great-grandkids. We look at the junk and we close the door and walk out. We pretend the problem doesn't exist.

I've done this same thing many times with my office. Stacks of paperwork spring up all around me. I do my best to ignore them, but then they scream out so loud that I have to take action. The problem—and this is a core problem of clutter—is that ignoring the problem is impossible. When I choose to try to work in my office when the clutter is growing, I feel this looming angst, particularly when I need to find something that is buried in one of those piles. Clutter is not neutral. It wears on me, needling away on at my sense of peace and my ability to move forward.

Clutter, particularly in our spaces and our schedules saps our energy, leaving us exhausted.

[　]

Now, we have finally committed to tackling the basement project, going through those mountains one by one. One major pile is earmarked for the trash, another for our favorite thrift store. Finally, we decided to keep a still-large pile. I suspect that one day we will declutter again and rid ourselves of half of what we choose to keep today.

I am admittedly no expert when it comes to decluttering. I know what to do but have a problem doing it. This is partly because I hate the process (although I love the end result). I also suffer from being overly frugal, so giving away perfectly good items is painful. Then there is the problem of decluttering by committee. Things I am happy to give away, Weezie wants to keep. Things that she wants to give away (incredibly valuable golf paraphernalia), I clutch tightly. Except for those whose internal wiring naturally leans to clean, open spaces, decluttering is a challenge.

Still, if we neglect the distasteful task, the clutter will grow and infringe on all of the other good work we are doing to create margin.

[ ]

Before we dive into the weeds of decluttering, we need to delve deeper and ask why we allow our lives to get this way. Granted, some of the issue is our culture and all its allure. We receive mountains of paperwork and piles of catalogs. We are inundated with requests for our time and money, and enticing toys begging for us to purchase them. The culture around us is wired to create clutter. The voices around us lure us to never say no, to never be satisfied.

The place I go to hear a different voice is Psalm 23. Right from the very first verse, David calls out the source of our issue. He paints a vivid picture of contentment.

> The LORD is my shepherd; I have all that I need. (Ps. 23:1 NLT)
> He makes me lie down in green pastures, he leads me beside quiet waters, he refreshes my soul. (vv. 1–3).

When I meditate on these words, I realize that much of my striving and acquiring reflects discontentment with what God has provided. I am convicted that, at the core, the way I live communicates:

> "The LORD is my Shepherd; I have all that I need, . . . *but I still want a whole lot more.*
>
> He makes me lie down in green pastures, . . . *but I keep on getting up because I have so much to do.*
>
> He leads me beside quiet waters . . . *but I pass right by because I might miss out on too much fun.*
>
> He restores my soul . . . *but I am still not satisfied.* I will *never* be satisfied!"

We have to take a risk. At some point, we either keep on filling every moment, filling every drawer, and spending every penny, or we create some space and find out whether God will fill the void. We are in a strong current, a virtual riptide, pulling us away from one another and away from God. Unless we are willing to be courageous and take the risk to swim out of the current and live countercul-turally, we will never find out whether God is enough to meet our needs.

As we move forward, gleaning the best ways and tactics with which to declutter our spaces and schedules, I encourage us to ask the hard question, "Do I want to change?" If so, God will meet us in our effort. God says, "Come, all who are thirsty, come to the waters; and you who have no money, come, buy and eat! Come, buy wine and milk without money and without cost. Why spend money on what is not bread, and your labor on what does not satisfy? Listen, listen to me, and eat what is good, and you will delight in the richest of fare" (Isa. 55:1–2).

At the heart, decluttering is a proclamation of contentment with what we already have. So, let's step out of the current and reclaim our freedom from overload.

BREATHING EXERCISE

Meditate each day for the next week on Psalm 23. Drink in the images. Reflect on how it would feel if this psalm described your life.

Decluttering Our Spaces

Time to roll up our sleeves and get practical and tactical. While I will defer to other experts on the best path to declutter, I have found a few practices particularly helpful in moving in the right direction. The overall method that has worked best for me is the "toss it, give it away, put it in its place" methodology.

Toss It

Much of what occupies our space, our time, and our calendars can simply be tossed. So many areas of our lives need pruning, but we will address three major culprits here: *possessions, schedules,* and *technology.* Our attics and basements are filled with stuff that no one would ever want to use. Our closets have items in them so old and so worn-out as to not be worthy of the Salvation Army. We sense how hard the task is when we realize the emotional attachment we have to things that are of no value. I have found that often I have to go through the same space three or four times because the first time around I cannot part with half of the things I should happily discard. And then there is technology. I have a box full of electrical accoutrements that once glittered but now have faded. It takes all of my willpower to let something that is not broken go, but that is precisely what I need to do.

Give It Away

It is easy to see how "give it away" applies to the things in our life. So many of us have piles of decent clothes that we no longer wear regularly that can be given away. The same goes for sporting goods, furniture, and every category in which we are prone to excess accumulation. Even though we know that we no longer need them, we find it hard to force ourselves to give away things that still seem to have life in them. What happens if we find we need them right after we have given them away?

I find it helpful to have a different paradigm in play when it comes to giving things away. If we begin to think of our "things" as having two or three lives, we are more likely to send our hand-me-downs to their next life. There is its first life, with us as its purchaser. When we use up its good first life, we give it away to someone who then enjoys a solid second life out of it. Who knows? Maybe that person will give it away to someone else, and it will have a third life. Beyond this, if we utilize a good, charitable thrift store for our giveaways, the proceeds can be used to fund some useful need. Either way, if we begin to ask whether we should give something away or not, and whether it is better to sit unused or rarely used in our overly cluttered house, or be newly enjoyed by someone who cannot afford the same item new, it frees us up to be more generous in our giving. I cannot think of a single item, in all the years we have employed this thinking, that we regretted giving away. Not one!

Put It in Its Right Place

After we have done the hard work of tossing the items that need to be tossed and giving away the articles that need to be given away, the hard work begins of putting the remaining items in their right place. This is when I realize that my first effort at decluttering did not go deep enough. When I face the fact that I have tossed and given away and still do not have room for what is left over, I am stuck with admitting that I am too attached to my possessions. So, I start over, tossing and giving until my space brings life instead of creating stress.

BREATHING EXERCISE

Give away one item this week.

Decluttering Our Schedules

While our spaces create tremendous clutter, we usually can work around the clutter without completely disrupting our lives. Someone at my office once commented on my "piling" system. I am able to stack excess things in a corner for a while, but the same does not hold true with my schedule. When our schedules are overloaded, we are overloaded. I am blown away by the crazy pace that so many people keep. I don't know why I am so surprised, since I did the same thing for so many years, and still struggle with it weekly. When it comes to our schedules, we lose perspective. We become blind to the breakneck speed at which we operate. We convince ourselves that we don't have any choice, no room to adjust, when we have much more control than we think. Unless we do the demolition work with our cluttered schedules, then renovation is a fantasy.

For so many years I suffered under the delusion that if I could only be more efficient and more disciplined, my schedule would be more sustainable. But too much is always too much, and all the efficiency in the world is only going to serve as a Band-Aid to my proclivity to take on too many commitments.

A recent bestseller, *The Four-Hour Workweek* by Tim Ferriss, describes the radical process the author went through to whittle his workweek down to just four hours a week. Ironically, he asserts that he accomplishes more in just four hours than he was accomplishing in over forty hours before he began the process. While we may not have the flexibility with our schedules to be as radical as Ferriss, the principle remains that laser focus in a few crucial areas will accomplish more than generalized activity in many areas.

Perhaps a starting point in our effort to declutter our schedules is naming a few of the areas where we are prone to lose perspective. Of course, this is personal to each one of us, but perhaps a few suggestions will spark other ideas that fit your situation.

Work

Our need to work is inevitable. Work is good. Work brings purpose to us, and the needed paycheck. The problem these days with work is its ever-expanding, pervasive nature. Despite all the technological efficiencies of today, perhaps because of them, we work longer hours than ever. Since so many households are two-income families, the implications of work balance are doubled from the experiences of previous generations. All of this is fine when kept in perspective. The key is to be honest about where we have lost perspective. As with other areas, my answers may not fit you, just as your answers won't fit me. Still, we need to ask the tough questions if we want to make progress.

- Am I comfortable with the hours I spend at work each week?
- Am I comfortable with the travel requirements of my job?
- Is it necessary for me to bring my work home as much as I do?
- Do I actually need to work at night? On weekends? While on vacation?
- What are a few concrete steps I could take to bring my work schedule into a better balance?

If this area is your primary stumbling block in your effort to create space, then profound soul-searching is in order. This may entail personal reflection on values and identity. It may take conversations with others on budget and lifestyle. You may need to have hard talks with your boss or supervisor. The problem may not be easy to solve, but if God is the architect of both purpose and rest, then a way can be found. Commit to finding a way, no matter what it takes. Use wise counselors and fervent prayer. God is not the author of overloaded, overwhelmed, stressed-out living.

Children's Activities

In our culture, one of the worst culprits, which I hesitate to mention, is children's activities. The movement toward travel sports has become ubiquitous. Travel sports impinge on ever-disappearing free time, cost inordinate sums of money, exhaust parents and kids alike, and rarely end up providing any long-term substantial benefit. Our kids might be slightly better equipped for high school sports, but rarely will advance to college-level competition, and even more rarely will advance to the point of professional proficiency. Even with some of the most gifted athletes, the whole travel experience of youth sports often produces a burnout that undermines the very advantage intended. We rationalize the choice by focusing on all of the advantages socially and through learning to compete hard, but many ways exist to achieve these ends without the extreme of travel sports. We justify this overcommitment because our kids love the sport. We claim that they are driving the choice. Exactly the problem! We cannot expect our kids to always discern what is best for them. They are not looking ahead, except in a dreamy way, and they often cannot imagine what it would feel like to have actual free time on their hands.

If you disagree with what I have written here, I understand and respect that disagreement. As long as we are able to have civil, honest conversations, we all benefit.

Youth sports are not the only violators. Music lessons, drama, and chess teams are often just as bad as sports.

One experience stands out in my mind. My son Alex was a competitive golfer. One summer, we traveled to a golf tournament for those hoping to play college golf. As I was at the range with Alex, we both could not help but notice several kids with dads hovering around them, correcting every swing. The misery on the kids' faces was evident.

This is not to say that all travel sports or youth leagues are wrong. In some cases, with great discernment, the choice may be a good one. I have special memories of coaching my kids in youth sports. We chose to live with the tension of how much is too much. Sometimes we erred on the side of too much. These were the early days of learning about margin, so we often got it wrong and then spent our energy trying to regroup and catch our breath. We tried to err on the side of less is more, but frankly, the "everyone else is doing it" mentality often resulted in poor decisions. These decisions regarding our children are too important for finger-wagging judgments. You and I cannot sequester our families from the good opportunities that exist today. My encouragement is to pause and consider all of the options, the impact on the family, and make the wisest choice possible in an imperfect world.

Church Commitments

The church has become one of the worst offenders of excess activity. It is so easy for the church to fall prey to the consumer culture, which says we have to be everything to everyone and offer every opportunity conceivable. Many churches have activities planned every night of the week, staffed by overloaded staff members and overextended volunteers, luring the congregation into the snare of breathless excess. Since it is all good stuff, who can complain? Churches need to do their own soul-searching. Are we feeding our congregations or choking our congregations?

Change

The list could go on and on. In the end, it is very personal, with not-so-easy answers. But the need to cull our schedules is dramatic. We cannot keep on going the pace we are going without serious fallout. The fallout will not likely come with lots of warning. Fallout comes suddenly in the form of relational breakdown, emotional fragility, and physical illness. Radical surgery is needed—before the storms hit and before the burnout or breakdown occurs.

Nothing will change unless something changes. If we are serious about wanting to live better lives with more space to breathe, then we will have to make difficult choices. At first, it will seem impossible. Once those choices are made, though, we will wonder why they seemed so difficult in the first place. Be bold. Be courageous. We have so much to gain.

Confession

This has been a difficult chapter to write because I fear that I have edged into being judgmental. That is not my desire or intention. Life is too hard and situations too complex for me to sit and judge. My real hope is to provoke meaningful dialogue about complex issues that often create guilt and regularly make margin seem unattainable.

BREATHING EXERCISE

Do an inventory of the time commitments in your life. Rate them from 1 to 10, with 1 being "a waste of time" and 10 being "can't live without." Are there any obvious decisions to be made?

Spacious Places

On the opposite side of decluttering are special places that become havens of joy and life. The aim is not to become minimalist; the goal is spaciousness with purpose.

What is the most beautiful place you have ever been? What made it beautiful? What feelings did that place evoke for you?

I have several favorite places. One is the beach in Sandestin, Florida. At sunset, when the temperature cools and the crowds lighten, the sun slowly fades over the horizon. Quiet orange rays color the sand and surrounding buildings. When I am there, I cannot help but take a deep, relaxed breath. Stress fades. Peace gently fills the space.

Beautiful places affect us in ways that defy logic. I think that I should be able to write well regardless of the environment, but I know from experience that place influences creativity. The same is true of relationships. I should be able to have an intimate, quality conversation at McDonald's, but I know that a nice restaurant with a soothing ambience enhances time spent with people I love.

The places where we spend our days enhance or detract from our experiences. The Bible captures a few images that we can claim in our effort to renovate our spaces. As we name our places and design our spaces, we have the opportunity to change the tenor of our experiences.

Sanctuary

The textbook definition of *sanctuary* is "a consecrated place."[2] A sanctuary is a set-apart place for worship and rest.

Where is your sanctuary? Have you designated and set apart a place that is for your worship, your reflection, your rest? The place doesn't need to be large or elaborate. It can be a special chair. The more we are able to set aside a place, the better. Some people dress their sanctuaries with candles or a favorite blanket. I know a lot of men will sneer at this sort of soft thinking, but men need their places too. When we claim this place and set it aside, our bodies begin to adapt and lean into our special place. We sit down with a cup of coffee and our Bibles, and our blood pressure lowers. A sanctuary is a place God meets us. Yes, He is with us everywhere, but Scripture also highlights the special presence of the Lord in the sanctuary. Listening to God is hard enough without battling extra distractions. A sanctuary graces us with room to breathe and space to grow.

If you don't have your own personal sanctuary, think about where you might create one. What do you need to do to set it apart? What will make it special? Like practicing the Sabbath, choosing a sanctuary can be a monumental step toward more joyful and peaceful living.

Your Hidden Sanctuary

I love to find ordinary ways in everyday life where I can gain an edge. One of those that I have enjoyed for a long time now is having a hidden sanctuary. Rarely a day goes by that I am not in my hidden sanctuary. I pray in my hidden sanctuary. I worship. I think and reflect. God meets me in my hidden sanctuary. My hidden sanctuary is my car.

For most people a car is the opposite of a sanctuary. A car is where road rage happens, blood pressure rises, stress increases. But it doesn't have to be that way. A paradigm shift is possible. Much of the time in my car is by myself. I control what speed I drive. I control what, if anything, I listen to. My time in my car is a built-in pause between activities.

I am not legalistic about my hidden sanctuary. Sometimes I make phone calls or listen to the radio. But most of the time I drive in silence. Occasionally I play worship music. On busy days, my car provides the necessary respite in between chaotic craziness.

I am not trying to be super-spiritual here. This is intensely practical. I need my hidden sanctuary to survive, even to prosper. Think about all of the time that you spend in your hidden sanctuary. Think of the opportunity available to you. Even for parents with children, the car can be transformed with a little thought. Maybe not every trip, but some trips.

The average commute time in the US is twenty-six minutes, one way. Almost an hour coming and going. Add other miscellaneous trips to this, and we see how great an opportunity awaits us in our hidden sanctuary.

This will take a total mind shift for many people. Instead of being a hated place of stress, we are creating a welcomed place of rest. The crazy thing is that it is all in the mind. When I first thought about this, it was like a major aha moment. I paused and realized I didn't have to rush. I didn't have to turn on the radio. I didn't have to tense up because of the other drivers. I had a choice. Now, not always, driving is fine, even enjoyable.

Life is hectic. Why not take the challenge of turning your car into your hidden sanctuary.

Refuge

The Bible refers to God as our refuge and our strength (Ps. 46:1). He is our place of safety from the storm. Why not also create a refuge in our spaces? A refuge is a safe place to retreat from the stresses, noise, and frenetic pace of life. Our refuge may be the same as our sanctuary, but it can be different too. A bath or a shower can be a refuge. A garden can be a refuge, or a workshop. It is a place to get away from the storms. The key is to specifically designate your places of refuge. That way, when the storms come, you know where to hide.

No-Technology Zones

What if we designated a few places in our homes as no-technology zones? Families could benefit tremendously from this concept— once the furor dies down. The first place to consider is the dining room table. How much better all of our meals would be if the phone was nowhere in sight! This is an easy decision that will make a huge difference. One decision, endless fruit. Another idea is to declare a no-technology time zone. This is a set-aside time when technology is off. It might be after 9:00 p.m. until 6:00 a.m. Singles, couples, and large families would benefit from the guardrails of a no-technology time zone. Whether self-enforced or regulated through an app, it's hard to think of a downside to this practice.

Nature

I have to admit that I am a "fair-weather friend" when it comes to nature. When the weather is right and the sun is shining, I love the outdoors. But if the temperature has a little chill or is drizzling, I prefer the nice, temperature-controlled atmosphere inside.

Camping has never been my favorite activity. Why spend a lot of energy to be less comfortable? I know that is kind of pathetic, but I long for my comfortable bed with my Tempur-Pedic™ pillow.

Even though spending time in nature is not natural to me, I keep coming back to nature as a joy and a blessing.

We have a Llewellin setter named Champ who loves his daily walk. I say walk, but it is more like a sprint. As the afternoon lengthens, he begins to get excited, knowing his time is coming. If anyone in our family does anything to indicate that he or she might go outside, Champ goes wild, whimpering and spinning around in circles. When we open the door, he sprints outside on our appointed path, hardly looking back—a picture of unbridled joy. He bounds through tall grasses, smells the air for any unusual scent, and swims in the nearby lakes, even in the dead of winter. We walk about two to three miles. He runs about six miles, back and forth, a happy dog. He knows something about the special place of nature that many of us lose.

For some reason, I forget that I actually love the outdoors. I love the fresh air and the quiet. I love the beauty of the trees and the feel of the grass under my feet. Even better are those times that I am able to enjoy the ocean or the mountains.

When I think about it, I feel closer to God when I am outdoors. I breathe better. I relax more. Conversations with friends seem to be richer when they take place outdoors.

The Bible is replete with the glory of God displayed through nature. "When I look at the night sky and see the work of your fingers—the moon and the stars you set in place—what are mere mortals that you should think about them, human beings that you should care for them?" (Ps. 8:3–4 NLT). "I look up to the mountains—does my help come from there? My help comes from the LORD, who made heaven and earth!" (Ps. 121:1–2 NLT). Paul confidently asserted to the Romans that all people are without excuse when it comes to knowing God because "they know the truth about God because he has made it obvious to them. For ever since the world was created, people have seen the earth and sky. Through everything God made, they can clearly see his invisible qualities—his eternal power and divine nature" (Rom. 1:19–20 NLT). Is it possible that we see and hear less of God because we spend less time in His magnificent creation?

[ ]

When we create and enjoy these beautiful places, we are forming the opportunity for a better rhythm. If my busyness is interspersed with times of sanctuary, retreats to my refuge, and wanderings in nature, I am infinitely better off. If there are a few times when I am wrenched from my phone, I am more at peace.

BREATHING EXERCISE

Determine your sanctuary, refuge, and no-technology time zone. When will you breathe this week the fresh air of God's creation?

Key Takeaways

- Space gives context, helping us to make sense of chaos. Space makes life more livable.
- Our lack of space exposes our discontentment. Creating space grows contentment and builds trust in the One who can handle the overload.
- Decluttering applies to our spaces and our schedules. Here is a simple method. Make the intentional decision to take one of just three actions:
  - Toss it.
  - Give it away.
  - Put it in its right place.
- Address primary offenders within our schedules:
  - **Work:** What are a few concrete steps to bring work into better balance?
  - **Children's activities:** Examine and then resist the temptation to overschedule our children's lives.
  - **Church commitments:** Keep in balance the endless opportunities to serve within the church.
- Regarding clutter in our spaces and our schedules, remember that intentions are fine, but in the end, nothing will change unless something changes.

- As we declutter, we have the chance to create special places. These places bring beauty and joy to life.
  - **Sanctuary:** a set-apart place for worship, reflection, and rest.
  - **Your hidden sanctuary:** Our cars are a place that we can transform into a hidden sanctuary.
  - **Refuge:** a place of safety for when life spins out of control and we need to get away.
  - **No-Technology Zones.**
  - **Nature:** God's place to retreat and hear His voice. A forgotten haven for restoration.

[7]
Quieting Voices

The great omission in American life is solitude . . . that zone of time and space, free from the outside pressures, which is the incinerator of the spirit.

—Marya Mannes

One Behemoth Monster

When Richard Swenson wrote *Margin* in 1992, cell phones were in their infancy, the World Wide Web was just reaching the public, and email was practically brand-new. Swenson described the rising tide of margin-less living without even knowing the tidal wave that was forming on the horizon. It is hardly hyperbole to suggest that technology has exploded, changing every aspect of life today. We live in a world obsessed with technology. The only question is how we avoid being swallowed by this behemoth monster that each day is growing more powerful and consuming.

In December 2017, the World Health Organization classified "gaming disorder," obsessively playing video games, as a mental disorder. According to the NHSTA, more than 1,000 car crashes occurred daily, more than 3,000 people died, and over 350,000 people were injured in the last year because we can't seem to resist texting while driving, despite constant advertising and laws prohibiting it. I would like to play my self-righteous card now, but I still fall victim to the temptation. Hard as it is to believe, history would suggest that what we are experiencing now with technology is the tip of the iceberg. Technologies such as 5G, virtual reality, and artificial intelligence will clearly add to the realism and addictiveness of the technology we own.

Let me be honest here. I struggle with technology. I fight to resist the lure of social media every day. Like a true recovering addict, I create routines and habits to avoid being drawn in to unproductive, time-wasting, soul-sapping technology. I check email way too often. I pay too much attention to "likes" and "followers." I am embarrassed by my weakness because I preach about the "evils" often.

I also have experienced tastes of the freedom that comes when I gain victory over my obsessions. I feel the tension relax when I quiet and leave my phone in the other room. Perhaps because I struggle, I know what a big deal it is to gain control over this monster.

What we need more of is honest conversation and real encouragement and less condemnation so that we can move in the right direction. In so many ways I love technology. So much good has come from technological advances. I have no desire to go backward. As we work together to slay this multiheaded monster, I will offer practical suggestions and tips for how to gain some measure of control over technology today and technology to come. I will offer these thoughts as a fellow struggler, not as one who has conquered the problem. When I look at myself with regard to technology, I have to admit that if I were more in touch with the depths of my soul, technology would have less appeal.

When my daughter was turning one, we gave her a big stuffed elephant for her birthday. We had to help her unwrap the box, which was almost as big as she was, being just one. At first, the huge elephant terrified her. Once she settled down, she decided the box was more exciting than the elephant and proceeded to play endlessly with the box. The outside wrappings were more alluring than the inside gift. Decades ago, C. S. Lewis wrote, "It would seem that Our Lord finds our desires not too strong, but too weak. We are halfhearted creatures, fooling about with drink and sex and ambition when infinite joy is offered us, like an ignorant child who wants to go on making mud pies in a slum because he cannot imagine what is meant by the offer of a holiday at the sea. We are far too easily pleased."[1] I can only imagine that if he were living today, he would have added technology into his list of half-hearted desires we pursue at the expense of abundant joy.

BREATHING EXERCISE

What is your Achilles' heel, your weakness when it comes to technology? What one small step can you take to lessen its grip on you?

Go on an Information Diet

I am a sucker for a bowl full of anything. When I go to a Mexican restaurant and the waiter brings out a bowl of tortilla chips before the meal, I have no self-control. Or if I sit down to relax after a round of golf and the waiter brings out a bowl of snack mix, I'm done. I don't even particularly like snack mix! I have learned about myself that I need to control portions. Whatever the size of the plate, I will eat everything on it. If the plate is small and the portions are reasonable, I have a much better chance at self-control.

Information is like snack mix to me. It comes in big bowls, not in manageable portions. Between news, social media, blogs, podcasts, YouTube, newspapers, and TV, information doesn't stream in; it floods in! I believe information is good—in the right portion.

I know people (you probably do too) who are information junkies. They are addicted to information, whether it is political, entertainment, or self-help. It feels good to be learning and absorbing, but in reality, we can only absorb but so much. The rest only serves to clutter our minds, making it difficult to even use the information we retain.

I feel as if I am constantly walking that tightrope of too much of a good thing. I have to carefully decide when, how much, and what information I put on my plate. Otherwise, I get lured into the information overload trap.

Here are the ways that I personally keep my portions of information healthy:

- **Restrict the information fire hose in the first hour of the day.** The first hour of the day is precious and sets the tone for the rest of the day. If we open the floodgate too early, our minds and spirits become agitated and unfocused.

- **Limit your sources to ones that give life.** While I value learning from people who think differently than I, prudence suggests that I have to set limits on information that is disruptive internally. Personally, I particularly find this true when it comes to political information.

- **Watch your hot buttons.** Some areas of information, while not bad in and of themselves, push buttons that are unhealthy for me. Social media falls in that category. Instagram and Facebook may be fun, but often leave the impression that everyone else is living fantastic lives. Just as with food, I need to be aware of what tempts me to gorge.

- **Even with the best content, too much is always too much.** I know a few people who constantly read and listen to amazing new content on personal growth and leadership. I love learning from them. Yet, sometimes I take in so much good content that my brain hits overload. Even if I am able to intellectually absorb the content, I have no bandwidth left to actually put it into practice. In my information gluttony, I lose all the nutritional value. The bottom-line question is, Are we changing for the good? What a shame if too much good information keeps us from good living!

BREATHING EXERCISE

Take a moment and do a personal inventory of the information flow in your life. A little reflection can go a long way in improving each day.

- What needs to be eliminated or reduced?
- When do you need to restrict information flow (perhaps early morning and late at night)?
- What information brings life to you?
- Is the information in your life making you a better person?

The Law of Proximity

Do you ever wonder why we have such a hard time breaking our obsession with our smartphones? I believe the reason is what I call "the law of proximity." This law states, *"We give our attention to that which is closest to us."* It makes logical sense. We don't lose sleep over terrible atrocities in other countries, even though they are truly terrible. When tragedy strikes our neighbor, though, we are devastated. When our own family is impacted, we drop everything to attend to them. That which is close to us affects us the most.

Back to our smartphones. What could be closer to us than our smartphones? We carry them with us everywhere, attached to our hips or in our pockets. Most people sleep with them right by their beds. In terms of proximity, we would be hard-pressed to think of *anything* that is closer to us than our smartphones. Plus, they never argue with us. They entertain us. They fill our empty places. They help us stay in touch and become more productive. We depend on our smartphones! We love our smartphones!

Yet deep down we know something is not healthy about the degree of attachment we have with our phones. How can we change this? One effective tactic is to turn the law of proximity on its head. We detach from our smartphones for specific periods of the day and night. This may be painful at first because our addiction is deep. If so, take baby steps. Here are specific suggestions:

- **Charge your smartphone in another room.** Get an old-fashioned alarm clock if necessary. Late-night texts and notifications can wait until the morning. If you have kids for whom you need to be available, then use Do Not Disturb on your phone. It will still allow select calls and notifications through.
- **Put your smartphone in another room during meals.** If eating out, leave your smartphone in the car.
- **Turn off all but the most necessary notifications.** The buzz or ding of notifications act as a stimulant (think about Pavlov's dogs, who salivated when they heard a bell indicating dinner). When we turn off the notifications, we are saying to our phones, "I control you; you do not control me."
- **Try turning your phone all the way off when you need to focus (or relax).**

BREATHING EXERCISE

Implement one of the ideas listed above for one week.

Silence and Solitude

Learning to listen and turning down the volume is one thing; silence is another. Silence is loud. It is awkward and uncomfortable. Whole industries exist to help us avoid silence. Why is it so distasteful for so many? Because silence is first terrifying before it is peaceful. Because in silence we face a vast, empty chasm, not recognizing that this is the path to our souls.

Only the bravest people dare to challenge the silence. Silence exposes motive and brokenness. Just try being silent for an extra moment in a conversation and watch the other person squirm and say something he or she didn't intend to say. Silence gets to the heart of the matter, whatever matter it is.

Ecclesiastes asserts that there is "a time to be silent and a time to speak" (Eccl. 3:7). Isn't this true in the best of relationships? How beautiful it is to enjoy the presence of a loved one in silence. The silence communicates love, acceptance.

We learn through silence. "Be still, and know that I am God" (Ps. 46:10). "The LORD is in his holy temple; let all the earth be silent before him" (Hab. 2:20). We cannot listen when we are talking, only when we are silent. I have come to believe more and more that my inability to hear God speak reflects primarily my inability to quiet the competing voices buzzing around in my head. Occasionally God thunders, but mostly He whispers. It is when I am quiet that I hear that whisper.

Silence is an acquired taste, but oh, how exquisite the taste! Silence may be the language of loneliness and pain, but it is also the music of peace. Push past the uncomfortable silence and find the beauty of quiet. We learn to breathe again as we learn to dance between raucous laughter and reverent silence, between lingering and engaging.

How different we are today from a few generations ago! We are inundated at every turn with noise, mostly by our own choice. What was peace-inducing a few decades ago is now very uncomfortable to us: driving in silence, sitting in our apartments or homes without the TV on, exercising without earbuds. Many of us have forgotten how to be silent and how to be alone. We suffer from this forgotten practice. Blaise Pascal wrote in the year 1670, "I have discovered that all the unhappiness of men arises from one single fact, that they cannot sit quietly in their own chamber."[2] What would Pascal think today if he witnessed the invasion of noise into every space in our lives?

Calm and peace elude us. Gentle thoughtfulness has been replaced by frenetic rantings. One of the trends that is popular today is mindfulness, a valiant attempt to counteract the speed and noise of life. Interestingly, the winner of Apple's Best of 2018 award for new apps was Calm, which had more than forty million downloads. The app simply creates fifteen seconds of quiet, as if we need help from an app to quiet ourselves for a whopping fifteen seconds.

Our spirits are deeply affected by perpetual rushing. One commercial for a high-speed internet provider makes fun of anyone who wants slower. We have been conned into believing that if we are rushing, we must be important, since our time is so precious. Oh, the joys of a leisurely walk, or an extended meal with a friend, without the next obligation pressing us to wrap things up! Hurry creates constant tension. That is a miserable way to live.

Regular periods of silence and solitude are our natural wiring, but our culture has rewired our brains, making silence painful. We must do the hard work of rewiring them back again! The deeper places in our soul and the deeper places in God cannot be found amid constant noise. Henri Nouwen said plainly, "Without solitude, it is virtually impossible to live a spiritual life."[3] Seventeenth-century theologian François Fénelon asserted, "God does not cease speaking, but the noise of the creatures without, and of our passions within, deafens us, and stops our hearing. We must silence every creature, we must silence ourselves, to hear in the deep hush of the whole soul, the ineffable voice of the spouse. We must bend the ear, because it is a delicate voice, only heard by those who no longer hear anything else."[4] Slowly, beautifully, silence and solitude will reintroduce us to our souls. When we meet our souls again, life is not far behind.

BREATHING EXERCISE

Sit in a chair silently for fifteen minutes, doing nothing. Observe how you feel and what you think.

Learning to Listen

It would be reasonable to ask what a section on learning to listen has to do with creating space in our lives. Seems like apples and oranges. But it is not. I recently read the book *The Listening Life* by Adam McHugh and became aware of how poorly I listen throughout every arena of life. A few months ago, I went to an audiologist because I was convinced my hearing was deteriorating. She put me through all sorts of tests. Ready for my first hearing aid, I was surprised to be told that I had passed all the tests with flying colors. Then the audiologist said matter-of-factly, "You don't have a hearing problem. You have a listening problem." Ouch!

Of course, the core issue is the very issue that we are talking about throughout this book, a cluttered life and a cluttered mind.

We have lost the value of living in the present. When our minds are distracted, we are unable to listen. Lots of things subtly clutter our minds. We may be eating lunch with someone and thinking about the meeting that we have right after lunch. We may be distracted by something happening in our peripheral vision. Just yesterday, I was talking with Weezie in our bedroom when out of the corner of my eye I saw someone walking outside with something in his hand. My eyes veered for a brief moment to the left as we talked and I wondered, *Is that a golf club or a fishing pole?* Of course, Weezie noticed it immediately and turned around to see what I was looking at. I then had to explain that someone walking on the road with a fishing pole had distracted me. Eventually we got back to the conversation.

I am learning that I listen with my eyes. This is particularly true in restaurants and at parties. We have all had the experience at a party of talking with someone who is constantly looking all around while talking to us. The very clear message is that we are not as important and interesting as all of the other people around us. Because of the eyes, we know we are not being listened to. And so, I have begun to try to discipline my eyes as I listen. As I work on this, I realize that my ears are listening better because my eyes are focused. This then translates to better conversation.

Rushing impacts listening. I listen better when I am unrushed. So, compounding takes effect. When I am moving slowly, arriving early, not checking email, my spirit calms. Then, I am able to focus on the other person. The improvement in listening is not 10 percent but 200 percent. We cannot expect to rush around, driven by a million things to do and think, and it not affect the quality of our conversations and relationships with those we love the most.

Learning to listen goes beyond verbal conversations. Learning to listen also pertains to learning to listen to nature, listening to God, and learning to listen to ourselves. Quoted earlier, Romans 1:20 says, "For since the creation of the world God's invisible qualities—his eternal power and divine nature—have been clearly seen, being understood from what has been made, so that people are without excuse." In other words, nature is talking to us about God. Who hasn't been affected by taking a moment to look out over the ocean or felt humbled by a sky full of stars? Who hasn't felt uplifted in the midst of towering mountain ranges? We instinctively know that nature has a message. Unfortunately, we don't listen very well. Hummingbirds, flowers, beaches, turtles, wind, storms, sunshine, snow, all speak of life if we will only slow down and listen. Life is so much richer if we will allow ourselves to revel in God's creation.

So many of us are disillusioned by how hard it seems to be to listen to God. Our inability to listen reflects the constant noise that drowns Him out. It is like trying to hear someone at a rock concert. We have become so used to the noise in our heads that we don't even see the problem. All of life is interconnected. If we can't listen well to the person across the table from us without being distracted, how do we expect to be able to listen to God, whom we cannot see and who does not normally speak audibly. I believe that as I learn to listen to my wife with my eyes and ears, I will better be able to listen to God with my heart. Listening to God is not about technique; it is about our hearts.

And when we become better listeners, we will become more aware of what is going on inside of us. We will learn to reflect. We will learn to pay closer attention to our feelings, even our own body language. This positive self-awareness will then bleed into better relationships, a greater ability to work in our strengths, and a more intimate walk with God, who wants us to become our most authentic selves.

BREATHING EXERCISE

Choose a particular time with a friend or your spouse and intentionally give him or her your undivided attention. Listen with your body, with your eyes, and with your ears. Reflect on the experience.

Key Takeaways

- Technology is a behemoth monster that must be addressed if we hope to create space to breathe.
- One step is to go on an information diet.
  - Restrict the information fire hose in the first hour of the day.
  - Limit your sources to ones that give life.
  - Watch your hot buttons.
  - Even with the best content, too much is always too much.
- The law of proximity: We give our attention to that which is closest to us.
- Our phones are a problem because they are always so close to us.
- Defeat the law of proximity by turning it on its head.
  - Charge your smartphone in another room.
  - Put your phone in another room during meals.
  - Turn off all but the most necessary notifications.

- Try turning your phone all the way off when you need to focus (or relax).
- Developing the difficult discipline of silence and solitude creates new places for joy and peace to grow.
- Out of the practice of silence and solitude, we learn to listen better.

[PART THREE]

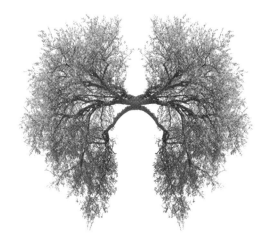

The New Path

[8]
A Beautiful Renovation

All that is not the love of God has no meaning for me. I can
truthfully say that I have no interest in anything but the love of
God which is in Christ Jesus. If God wants it to, my life will be
useful through my word and witness. If He wants it to, my life will
bear fruit through my prayers and sacrifices. But the usefulness
of my life is His concern, not mine. It would be indecent of me to
worry about that.

Dominique Voillaume as quoted in *The Signature of Jesus*[1]

Unwinding Stress

One of the habits I am trying to implement in my life is the
practice of deep breathing. Each day I take a few moments to
inhale deeply and exhale completely. Every time I do this, I am
acutely aware of the stress that I hold in my neck and in my shoulders. After several deep breaths, the stress unwinds a little. This is
one of my many stress Band-Aids.

If I weren't wired in overdrive, if I had a different, more laid-back
temperament, I might have never learned the lessons I have learned
or be sitting here writing this book. But I am. This has caused me to
delve deeply into this thing we call stress. What is stress?

Stress is a response to either internal thoughts or external stimuli.
For instance, I feel stress if I think my children are not well, whether
they are fine or not. I feel stress because of financial pressures,
whether those pressures are real or imagined. I feel stress when I feel
threatened. I feel stress when my identity is challenged, such as when

I speak in front of people. They may like what I say or fall asleep. In these cases, the situations themselves are not the problem; my mental response to the situation causes me stress.

External stimuli also cause stress. If I drive twenty-five miles per hour in a neighborhood, I probably won't feel stress. If I am rushed and driving too fast, then stress enters in. Rushing almost always creates stress, although I think we have become so used to stress that we are not even aware of its presence—until we take a deep breath and feel the tightness in our necks, shoulders, and backs. High-idling engines put stress on a vehicle. That stress may not show up today or tomorrow, but the stress will eventually cause a breakdown. Excess noise causes stress. Ask any mother of small children. Lack of clarity causes stress.

Stress is a response, a barometer of our lives. If stress-free living were our only objective, we could hide away in some remote place, avoiding people (major stress inducers), and while away the hours. That might work, but it would be a terrible way to live this gift that God has given us. Jesus said that He came to give us abundant life (see John 10:10 NKJV), not an easy life. Breathing again is a function of living God's way, not carefully orchestrating life (as if we can do that) to avoid anything that might raise our blood pressure.

This has been the high goal of this book: to expose the ways of the world that feed stress, with no corresponding gain, and to reintroduce God's old ways that reduce stress regardless of culture. God's ways are timeless.

With this in mind, let's review the actions and mindset that will aid us in our efforts against undue stress.

- Assess your life. Where are you right now? What is working and what is not working? What brings about stress in your life? What are your hot buttons?
- Identify the fears you fight and the lies you cling to that are keeping you trapped in an endless cycle of overload.

- Name the forms of overload that are your weakness, whether accumulation, opportunity, or distraction. Be specific.
- Create a frame for your day, a morning and an evening routine, that enables you to enter each day with clarity and freshness.
- Learn to slow down. This includes both the speed with which you plow through your days and inserting pleasant pauses into each day.
- Develop slow living habits and practices, such as reading, unrushed dining, and walks.
- Put work in its right place in your life.
- Find your delightful rhythm for each day.
- Start practicing the Sabbath, one day a week in honor and obedience to God, for your enjoyment.
- Wrangle technology so that it serves you rather than you serving it.

All of these steps and practices are ways of right-sizing life. This is what Henri Nouwen suggested when he said that discipline is creating space where God can act. When we step back and get control of these forces that work against us, we open space for those we love, and we open space for God. This is the end goal: love—love for God and love for one another. In the end, if we only create space so that we are able to live more successful, comfortable lives, we are missing the beauty that is there for the asking, there for the seeking.

BREATHING EXERCISE

Determine that it is possible to reduce stress in your life. Pick one of the options listed above and put it into practice this week.

Prioritizing Relationships

We are now on our way to a beautiful life renovation. For some, the work put in so far has created a small glimmer of hope. For others, new shoots are springing up as we free time, create space, and quiet the harassing voices. As I learned almost thirty years ago, progress—not perfection—is the goal. We cannot undo a lifetime of patterns overnight. What we can do is begin to live spacious lives, lives in which we breathe easily.

When we began renovating our kitchen, we had a vision of what the space could become, but I don't think we had any idea of how magnificent the transfiguration would be. Renovations have a few common characteristics.

- **Renovations simplify.** We went from cluttered to clean. We know now where everything is, partly because we have fewer things in our kitchen. Everything has a place and a purpose.
- **Renovations freshen.** With our kitchen, we didn't add a single square foot, but we feel as though we have an entirely fresh new space. We went from slightly anxious when we entered our dysfunctional kitchen to a feeling of contentedness now.
- **Renovations create opportunities.** For years, we hesitated slightly when it came to entertaining because our space was so unenjoyable to us. With the new renovations, we bring more people into our home. That's not because we think they care whether our kitchen is renovated or not, but because we enjoy our kitchen more and want to share it with others. This is one of the wonderful fruits of renovation. We now have space for people. Because we can breathe, we are drawn to share that with others. Out of margin, we have life to give to others. We are in a world of frazzled, overloaded, stressed-out people who desperately need to see and touch a differ-

ent way of living. Words, like this book, are a small step but pale next to the living example of a renovated life. Out of a breath-filled life, we have the space to give priority to the Great Commandment, to love God (Matt. 22:37), and the companion commandment to love our neighbors. When we are so busy, so rushed, that we can't catch our breath, our neighbors fall victim to our hurry.

Not Meant to Be Alone

A recent popular worship song playing now is entitled "Only Jesus" by Brian and Jenn Johnson. I love the song and the sentiment behind it. Without meaning to be critical, underlying the words of the song is a problem. God created us for relationship with one another. He never intended to be our "only" relationship. We experience the love of God directly from Him and through the vessel of other people. He speaks to us through His Word and through His church, which is composed of other people. God created us for relationship!

In case you are not completely convinced, let's go all the way back to the beginning. God created the world in six days and gave us the gift of the Sabbath on the seventh day. Six times in Genesis 1, we read that what God had created was "good" (vv. 4, 10, 12, 18, 21, 25). Then, after He had created man, male and female, He stepped back and saw that it was all "very good" (v. 31). From there, Genesis goes into the more detailed description of the creation of man and woman in the garden of Eden. In the beginning it was just the man and God. No one else. Without any prompting from Adam, any complaint, God then said, "It is not good for the man to be alone" (Gen. 2:18). Think about this for a moment. The first time in all creation anything was not good was the aloneness of man. Not only was this the first time anything was called "not good," but the not-good thing existed in the garden of Eden. It is as if Genesis is making a huge exclamation point around this crucial thought. Here is the progression: Good, good, good, good, good, good, very good, not good!

God is in relationship—Father, Son, and Holy Spirit—and He created us for relationship. While the relationship between a man and a woman in marriage is a special form of relationship that God blesses, the whole of Scripture makes clear that all kinds of relationships garner the blessing of God. Deep friendships like that of David and Jonathan. The three close disciples to Jesus, and the Twelve. The church, described as the body of Christ. "By this everyone will know that you are my disciples, if you love one another" (John 13:35). We are not meant to be alone!

What does this have to do with learning to breathe again? We create space in our lives to make space for what God intended. If we were to create space in our lives without at the same time making space for the priority of relationship, we would be creating a counterfeit good that would simply leave us empty. In renovating of our lives by redeeming time, quieting noise, and creating space, we create the soil in which relationships can blossom.

Clearly, this is God's good intention that has become a victim to the fall. Relationships are messy, dysfunctional, hurtful, and often abusive. Too many people suffer from suffocating loneliness. Still, relationship is precisely what God deeply desires to redeem and make beautiful again. This is the intended fruit of learning to breathe again. Equally, relationships are one of the most disastrous victims of the frenetic overload that is normal in our culture today. We no longer relate to each other except through the medium of our phones, and through social media. The negative future consequences of our present disconnectedness may exceed anything we can imagine.

To this end, we seek to replace the clutter of today with meaningful, fulfilling relationship. This is what God intended from the very beginning.

The Power of Two

Never has our culture been more connected and yet, more isolated at the same time. We have seemingly infinite ways of staying in touch with one another and no inclination to understand each other. The end result is surface relationships and deep loneliness.

Casual relationships and social media contacts can be tons of fun and great ways of staying in touch with lots of people. But they do not replace close, intimate, face-to-face relationships. Ecclesiastes says, "Two are better than one . . . If either of them falls down, one can help the other up. But pity anyone who falls and has no one to help them up" (Eccles. 4:9–10).

Over the last few years, struggling through Perrin's cancer and the ensuing grief, we have been recipients of overwhelming love and care. We could not have survived without the countless acts of love. On a deeper level, though, a few very close friends carried me when I couldn't carry myself. These friends were my strength, my faith, my courage, and my solace. Deep friendships, established way before the storm clouds showed on the horizon, have shared insight, expressed love, and borne unbearable burdens. They have been the joy of life for decades now.

I talk to people almost every day who have many friendships but no one with whom they can share their hearts and souls. Men are the worst about this, but I suspect that many women also suffer from superficiality in their varied relationships.

The power of two choosing to share life on a soul level together defies imagination. The very best of life is experienced in relation-ship. As my years go on, I realize more and more that accomplish-ments and acquisitions do not satisfy the spirit. No matter how much I want to achieve great things and make a difference in the world, my heart resonates when I am understood and loved for who I am.

The choice to risk and invest in deep, personal relationships may be the most important decision you make this year. The impact of the power of two people intentionally choosing to walk through life together, compounded over ten, twenty, thirty, or more years, will make us different people. If you already are in this kind of relationship, consider choosing to take it to the next level through increased transparency and vulnerability.

BREATHING EXERCISE

Assess the state of relationships in your life: acquaintances, groups, and closest friendships. What is one step you can take to give higher priority to relationships?.

Putting It All Together

Our kitchen is renovated now. It's been several years, and we are still thoroughly enjoying the new space each day. We renovated part of the basement also. While still in the midst of decluttering the other half of the basement, we can see the light at the end of the tunnel. This past year, we replaced old, cloudy windows whose seals had broken. In the next few years, we hope to work on the upstairs.

Just a few years back, we were so frustrated with our house that we were ready to move. We loved so much about the house, but the massive job ahead of us and the constant frustration of overwhelming clutter almost caused us to throw in the towel. I am so thankful that we did not give in.

Like our lives, renovation is constant. It is a process, not a destination. Renovated lives full of purpose and joy are possible, even in our frenetic, distracted, stressed society. We begin by demolishing all of the strongholds our culture continues to plant in our lives. We look inside to see how we have participated in our overwhelmed existence. We challenge the world's answers to happiness. Then we use the newfound space to infuse purpose, to prioritize people, and to reignite the flame of our love for our Lord and Maker.

Renovation is possible. We control a lot more than we think. We control what time we get up in the morning. That sets the tone. We control to the greatest extent when we leave the house and what we do in the car. We plan our days and outline our highest priorities. We choose a few periods in the day that we are unplugged. We choose not to rush.

We may choose not to get up early. We may choose not to turn off notifications. We may choose to stay up late watching the football game. But those are our choices. And our consequences. When we look at this mountain that we call overload, let's admit that much of the mountain is of our own making. We know the culture around us is not helping in the slightest, but we still can make real headway. And as we get a sense that life can be different, we continue to chip away and make even more progress.

Here's to small steps in the right direction!

Here's to creating space to breathe again!

BREATHING EXERCISE

Write an "imagine" document. Imagine life five years from now if you address the overload in your life and learn to breathe again. Write a paragraph for each of the following areas about how life will be different: your schedule, your relationships, your spiritual life, your enjoyment, your impact on others.

Key Takeaways

- Stress is a response to either internal thoughts or external stimuli. Stress is a barometer of our lives.
- It is possible to reduce stress by changing our practices that invite stress and changing our mindset that feeds stress.
- We create space for love, love for God and love for one another.

- Relationships are a fountain of joy enabling calm in the storms. They are worth our highest priority.
- Within the breadth of relationships, the power of a few closest friends stands out. These friendships will help us navigate the hard times and urge us to grow deeper with God. These relationships are God's gift.
- Despite the strong current of culture luring us into overload, creating a spacious, renovated life is possible, step-by-step, day by day.

[Epilogue]
Breathing in Every Season

I vividly remember many years ago teaching a series of classes on "Learning to Breathe Again" to an extremely diverse class. The class was comprised of every age group and walk of life. Men who were working and men who had retired. Men climbing the corporate ladder and men in routine, demanding jobs. Women who were stay-at-home moms and women who were single moms working and managing a full household. Couples with young children and couples getting ready to leap into marriage.

At first I was totally intimidated. I wondered whether I was in over my head and if the message and encouragement of these lessons could possibly speak to all these different walks of life. Frankly, I thought I might get eaten alive. An amazing thing happened. From the beginning I could viscerally see that all of these different people in various seasons of life struggled with these issues. Certainly the intensity of struggle in some situations and seasons was more intense than others, but everyone shared the common issues. The struggle was the same, but the application of the principles varied, depending on the situation. And so, it is worthwhile to give attention to unique difficulties that come at various times of life, and how *Space to Breathe Again* might be creatively practiced in those seasons. Even if your season is a little different from the ones described below, the discussion may spark your creativity in applying the principles to your situation. Let's consider a few together:

20-something, single, just entering adulthood and the workforce:

The struggles of this season are unique. This is a high-energy season filled with possibility and opportunity. There are places to go, people to see, money to make, fun to experience. The picture is exciting but overwhelming. Sometimes those in this season have the hardest time embracing the problems that come with overload. Yes, they are exhausted, but it is a good exhaustion, an exciting exhaustion, not a problem. Deep down they know they are going too fast, but what's the harm? Sure, social media can become obsessive, but everyone's doing it, and no one is disciplining it, or so it seems. Burnout seems a distant threat.

Some of this is absolutely true. Youth offers opportunity that should be grabbed with gusto. Cautious, controlled lives are boring and dull. The problem is these early years create patterns that may be survivable today but will sink us tomorrow. This is precisely the season to establish a few critical principles that can free us in life-giving ways and sustain us as we move into different seasons. These principles set the tone for future health.

First, focus on foundations. Establish great firsts in your life for the future. Though income may be low, discretionary money may be higher. I remember my first job, making $12,000 a year. The bad news was that this didn't stretch very far. The good news was that my tithe of $100 per month did not break the bank. This is the season to establish your first hour with God. It may be hard, but deal with it, you are strong.

Next, throttle technology now before addiction sets in. Get as creative as necessary, but tame that beast. It will never get easier. Set reasonable, healthy limits to the place and time of technology in your life and be vigilant. This will give you a fighting chance as technology seeks a bigger place in years to come. Embrace a healthy balance. Leave your phone in your car or another room during meals. Have a "cutoff time" when the phone is cut off. Enjoy social media, but don't be consumed with it.

Finally, prioritize real relationship. Lean toward face to face over text. Begin to establish deep friendships and relationships on a foundation of honesty and vulnerability. Find a mentor. If you prioritize face-to-face relationships, you will find that you don't have time to waste with the fluff that defines so many relationships today.

If you do these few things, you will have such a massive head start on creating the space in which you can breathe. The good habits of first foundations, tamed technology, and real relationships set the trajectory that will be enjoyed for decades to come.

Parenting small children

This is truly one of the most demanding seasons in which to practice any sort of margin. Kids want all of our attention and then some. The days with young children start obscenely early, and even if they go to bed early, nothing is left in the parent's tank. In addition, the demands of careers and unending commitments are never higher. Add to this our culture's insistence that we give our children every opportunity possible. This consumes afternoons, nights, weekends, and more. Any resistance to opportunity borders on abuse. How do we have a prayer of breathing in this season?

First, give yourself huge doses of grace. Perfect is not possible. Your choices as a parent will necessitate compromises. The key is to take advantage of the low-hanging fruit. Gain the victories where you can so the compromises don't overwhelm you.

Consider the major categories of time and commitments and be stingy and intentional about saying yes and no. Work hard to get ahead of the curve on important decisions so impulse doesn't win the day. Particularly, consider these areas:

- *Decide the place technology will play in your children's lives and your family's life.* Err on the side of less.
- *Choose only a few commitments when it comes to your children's time.* Know that opportunities like sports requiring travel will suck you dry both in time and money. Unless your child is truly a prodigy, and maybe not even then, choose other ways to keep your child involved in fun sports. Not every minute of their time has to be scheduled. Once you get started, it is really hard to stop.

- *Practice single attention.* When you are with your spouse, be fully with your spouse. When you are playing with the kids, give them your full attention. You are modeling ways that will become a deep part of their lives. What a gift attention is to those we love!
- *Decide how your family will practice the Sabbath.* This is one time you can build in space to breathe, if you are vigilant and creative. Practice the spirit of the Sabbath, even if you have to compromise on the rigid details of the Sabbath.
- *Work diligently to prioritize priorities.* Think through exactly what place work plays in your life now. Are there ways to be equally effective at work with a little less time invested?
- *In this season resist more than ever the lie that "more is better."* If ever there was a season in which less is truly better (and absolutely necessary), it is this season.
- *Keep God front and center in your own life.* This will be a tremendous challenge. Your time with God may be whittled down to fewer minutes than you would like, but do your best to give God your best.

Wilderness Seasons

Life can deliver brutal blows. As if it is not hard enough to attain a modicum of margin when everything is going well, each of us will go through times and seasons, some short and some interminably long, when life is not normal, and extreme measures are required. I certainly experienced this for almost a full decade.

Looking back on that season when my head barely stayed above water, I learned survival is victory. During the early weeks and months of Perrin's cancer, I had a vision of being a tower of strength and faith. In reality I was a teetering bucket of barely held together emotions. Each day I would gather myself in the morning, hoping I could somehow make it to the end of the day. Then I would fall into bed at the end and wake up to repeat the same pattern. I think

I probably put on a reasonably good exterior appearance when I needed to, but internally I couldn't imagine how I would make it through another day. Year after year went on that way, with slightly increasing stamina to handle days of meeting for scan results and figuring out what was next to stem the tide of pain. I didn't feel strong. I saw my weakness. In that weakness, God invisibly helped me up day after day. We survived! *Now, I recognize that surviving the wilderness is victory.*

That season was where the lessons expressed in this book went from self-improvement to soul-survival. Like Luther, the painful trials we faced daily required us to *expand daily disciplines*. Both Weezie and I depended on our early mornings to sit quietly and prepare for the day. In fact, we both increased the time in quiet and prayer. When the wilderness comes, even though the quiet can be louder than ever, hear the words of Isaiah: "In repentance and rest is your salvation, in quietness and trust is your strength" (Is. 30:15)

We learned that regardless of how bad it got, we needed to *find joy in some way each day*. Perrin made that easy because she was always smiling, always joyful. The simplest pleasure would cause her to exclaim, "That makes me so happy." We both realized that the intensity of our struggle was not sustainable. We encouraged and supported one another in any creative ways possible to find joy and de-stress in some manner each day, whether that was a round of golf, a massage, watching a comedy, or dinner with the right friends. The heaviness was always there, so we were proactive in finding joy in the midst of the trial.

We rehearsed regularly the goodness of God. We practiced the wisdom of Joseph Bayly: "Don't forget in the darkness what you learned in the light." We did this by regularly rehearsing what we knew to be true—the never-failing goodness of God—even though our emotions were crying out otherwise. We memorized Scriptures and poured time and again through the Psalms. In the wilderness season, we sought to let our minds inform our emotions.

[EPILOGUE]

Finally, in the wilderness seasons of life, *lean on your family and friends.* The wilderness is not a place to be alone. Let your friends and family be your courage when your courage is failing. Let them hold you up when your knees are buckling. Leaning on friends is not a sign of weakness but wise humility.

[Notes]

Introduction

1. Frank Kewis Dyer and Thomas Commerford Martin, *Edison: His Life and Inventions* (New York: Harper & Bros., 1910), 615–616.

Chapter 1

1. John Ortberg, "Ruthlessly Eliminate Hurry," *Christianity Today* (July 4, 2002), https://www.christianitytoday.com/pastors/2002/July-online-only/cln20704.html.
2. John Mark Comer, *The Ruthless Elimination of Hurry: How to Stay Emotionally Healthy and Spiritually Alive in the Chaos of the Modern World* (New York: Waterbrook, 2019), 19.
3. Richard A. Swenson, *Margin: Restoring Emotional, Physical, Financial, and Time Reserves to Overloaded Lives* (Colorado Springs, CO: NavPress, 2004), 69.
4. Ibid., 15.
5. file://Users/thomasthompson/OneDrive/Perrin/Despite%20Cancer%20God%20is%20Good%20-%20OnFaith.webarchive.
6. Andrew Weil, Breathing: The Master Key to Self Healing audiobook (Boulder, CO: SoundsTrue, 1999, 2001).
7. Belisa Vranich, *Breathe: The Simple, Revolutionary 14-Day Program to Improve Your Mental and Physical Health* (New York: St. Martin's Press, 2016), 12.
8. Ibid., 15.

Chapter 2

1. James Dobson, *What Wives Wish Their Husbands Knew About Women* (Colorado Springs, CO: Focus on the Family, 1975), 27.

2. Bruce Larson, *There's a Lot More to Health Than Not Being Sick* (Waco, TX: Word, 1981), 114.

Chapter 3

1. Gordon MacDonald, *Restoring Your Spiritual Passion* (Nashville, TN: Thomas Nelson, 1986), 24–25.

Chapter 4

1. *The Weight of Glory* by C. S. Lewis copyright © C. S. Lewis Pte. Ltd. 1949, Extract reprinted by permission.
2. *The Screwtape Letters* by C. S. Lewis copyright © C. S. Lewis Pte. Ltd. 1942, Extract reprinted by permission.
3. Calvin C. Newport, *Digital Minimalism: Choosing a Focused Life in a Noisy World* (New York: Portfolio, 2019).

Chapter 5

1. Stuart Brown, *Play: How It Shapes the Brain, Opens the Imagination, and Invigorates the Soul* (New York: Penguin, 2009), 6.

Chapter 6

1. Henri Nouwen, *A Spirituality of Living: The Henri Nouwen Spirituality Series* (Nashville, TN: UpperRoom, 2011), 16.
2. *Merriam-Webster Dictionary*, s.v. "sanctuary," https://www.merriam-webster.com/dictionary/sanctuary.

Chapter 7

1. *The Weight of Glory* by C. S. Lewis copyright © C. S. Lewis Pte. Ltd. 1949. Extract reprinted by permission.
2. Blaise Pascal, *Pensés, "Diversion,"* (New York: Penguin, 1966), 49.
3. Henri Nouwen, *Making All Things New* (San Francisco: Harper & Row, 1981), 69.
4. François Fénelon, *Christian Perfection*, trans. Mildred Whitney Stillman (Minneapolis: Bethany House, 1975), 155–56.

[Appendix]
Systems

Calendar Systems

- Do you have one central place where you keep all scheduled events/meetings/appointments?
- Is your calendar easily accessible to you wherever you are?
- Do you keep all events on your calendar?
- Do you miss or forget appointments?
- Do you have repeating appointments that make priority areas of your life move forward automatically?
- Do you block large chunks of time for priorities?

To-Do Systems

- Do you have a system for repeating tasks?
- Do you write down a to-do list for each day?
- Do you have a plan for each week?
- Do you plan out projects?

Information Systems

- Do you have a place for information you want to track or keep: passwords, favorite restaurants, books to read, great quotes, ideas, key documents?
- Do you have a system to keep technology in balance?

Financial Systems

- Do you have automated systems for paying bills on time?
- Do you have a budget and a system for keeping track of your budget?
- Do you have a system for regular giving?
- Do you have a system for regular investing?

Reflection Systems

- Do you have a regular time or times set aside for reflection?
- Do you set goals?
- Do you have a system to regularly review your goals?

Relational Systems

- Do you have a mentor?
- Do you mentor others?
- Do you have good friends and regular times to get together?

Spiritual Systems

- Do you spend regular time with God?
- Do you read/study/meditate on the Bible?
- Do you read spiritual-growth books?
- Do you go to worship regularly?
- Do you serve others?

Health Systems

- Do you block out time for exercise regularly?
- Are you eating in a way that you are comfortable with?

[About the Author]

Tommy Thompson is an accomplished entrepreneur, executive coach, and passionate teacher whose heart is to impact people for good and for God. After more than thirty years of owning and leading a wide variety of companies, Tommy is now an active blogger, executive coach, and consultant, while also leading a mentoring ministry at his church. He is married to Weezie and has two sons, Chris and Alex.

IF YOU ENJOYED THIS BOOK, PLEASE CONSIDER SHARING IT WITH OTHERS.

Recommend this book personally to friends and family, as well as to those in your small group, book club, workplace, and classes.

Mention the book in a blog post or on Twitter, or upload a photo of the cover with your positive review to Instagram, Facebook, and Pinterest.

Connect with the author on Facebook to express your appreciation for the book's message and, perhaps, how it had a positive effect on your life.

Order a copy of the book for someone you know who would be challenged and encouraged by its message.

Look for the book on Amazon.com and leave a positive review.

And visit us to see the many other books, products, and publishing services we offer.

CreativeEnterprisesStudio.com

1507 SHIRLEY WAY, SUITE A
BEDFORD, TX 76022-6737
ACREATIVESHOP@AOL.COM